PYTHON PROGRAMMING FOR INTERMEDIATES

The Ultimate Intermediate's Guide to Learn Python Programming Step by Step and Master Computer development + machine learning In A Few Days

(Vol. 2)

AUTHOR

BILL STEVEN

This document is geared towards providing exact and reliable information with regards to the topic and issue covered. The publication is sold with the idea that the publisher is not required to render accounting, officially permitted, or otherwise, qualified services. If advice is necessary, legal or professional, a practiced individual in the profession should be ordered.

- From a Declaration of Principles which was accepted and approved equally by a Committee of the American Bar Association and a Committee of Publishers and Associations.

Respective authors own all copyrights not held by the publisher.

Table of contents

Chapter 1. Introduction

What Is Python and Why Is It a Good Programming Language to Learn?

Learning a new programming language can be a great experience. You may want to learn it so you can know more things about your computer and understand how it works, how a website works, and perhaps you want to learn so you can create your applications and programs. If you have never worked with coding in the past, then it is hard to figure out how to get started. With a little search, you will notice that there are many coding languages available that you can work with besides Python. From Java to C++ and so much more, it's hard to determine which coding language is the best for you.

As a beginner who has never done anything with coding, Python is one of the best coding languages to work. Python has long been considered a beginner's language because it is so easy to learn, and you will be able to understand it right from the beginning. This is just one of the many reasons why you should choose to work with Python. You will also like there is a large active community devoted to this programming language and what's good is that it's open-source so you can get started without literally having to pay anything. This language will also work on any operating system, so it won't matter which computer you want to use the language on.

Despite being the coding language that beginners like to work with, this doesn't mean that there aren't a lot of advantages that come with working with this language. Python on its own is capable of writing great codes in the process, and you can also combine it with a few other languages so that you can create as many strings of code that you like. Now, let's take some time to look at Python and all the things that you need to know to get started on using this coding language.

Why should I learn Python?

As we mentioned before, there are a lot of different coding languages that you can learn about and use. So, if there are a lot of choices out there, why would you want to go with the Python coding language in the first place? Many people, both experts, and beginners all choose to go with Python because it is easy to learn, easy to read, and it is capable of creating large, challenging codes that you might want to write. There are a lot of different reasons that you would want to work with this coding language, and these include:

• Simple enough to read

You will find that Python is a programming language that is very easy to read, even if you are a beginner. When it is compared to some of the other coding languages, it is one of the most readable languages. Since this is a natural coding language to go with, many beginners like that they can catch on so quickly and that they will understand what they are doing in no time.

• Free

Another benefit of going with Python is that it is free to use. There are some computer coding languages that you would have to pay for so you can use them and this can be quite expensive, especially if you want to learn how to use more than one of them. Python is free to use, so you don't have to worry about this problem.

• Fast

Even though this language is natural enough for any beginner to learn, Python is still considered one of the high-level languages that you can learn. This means that when you make a program and generate your codes by using Python, you will see that the execution is friendly and quick. Some coding languages are harder to work with or can't go as fast as you want them to, but this is a problem you won't have when using Python.

• Works on a variety of platforms

You can work with the Python language no matter which platform you would like to use it on. Linux is the operating system that a lot of people will choose to go with, but you can still work with Python even if you are on a Windows or Mac computer. This is excellent news because it means that you can use Python without having to make any significant changes to your current setup.

- A big library to work with

Once you start to get familiar with Python, you will notice that it comes with an extensive library. This is good news for beginners because the library is what contains all the functions, codes and other things that you need to make the language work for you. This library will help make sure that you can do some useful stuff when trying to make your code.

- A large community

Whether you have worked with coding language in the past or not, it is nice to know that there is a large community of Python users that will help you out if you ever get stuck. Any time that you need some ideas like a new project or if you have a question, or if you want to learn something new, there is a library of information to provide you with the information that you need to help you get started.

Chapter 2. Working with Python

How Python Works

You know a handful of terms related to python, so let's take a step back for a second and talk about what makes python the way it is. It is an "object-oriented" programming language. To understand this, you should first know what functions are. Also known as subroutines or procedures, functions manipulate data and allow you to use code multiple times in a program without copying the code over and over again. Functions are front-and-centre when using a procedure-oriented style of programming, but it doesn't always work very well when you're writing more extensive programs. That's when object-oriented programming becomes more useful. Python does not prioritize functions, but it still uses them.

Objects and classes

When you combine data and function, you get an object. The Python Programiz website describes objects as a collection of data (variables) and function. In the real world, a car or house is an object. Just like every object needs a design or blueprint, every object in Python needs a class, and like design plans, classes contain all the information and details needed to create the object. That process of creation is called instantiation (which begins whenever you type in the keyword class) while the resulting object is known as an instance of a class. You use classes when you need to keep data related to each other organized and grouped.

Attributes and methods

Classes need functionality attached to them, or what's the point? You achieve functionality by setting attributes, which hold the data related to functions, which in Python are known as methods. Confused? Let's look at the example HackerEarth uses:

class Snake:

name: "diamondhead"

You just created a new class, Snake, and assigned the word "name" to the word "diamondhead." That makes sense visually. Whenever you want to refer back to this information, you want the program to know that the snake name is diamondhead. The class needs to be assigned to a variable, like so:

snake = Snake()

Now, you can retrieve the attribute, which in this case is diamondhead. We should first explain the dot notation, which is a literal dot or period. Using this tells Python to look inside the space that is before the dot. Whatever is inside the space is the code that Python should execute.

You would type in:

```
print(snake.name)
```

You just told Python to look at Snake, which leads it back to Snake (), which leads it back to the class you created. When you run this program, you end up with:

```
print(snake.name)
```

```
diamondhead
```

That's the essence of classes and methods. Methods are always associated with a class.

Inheritance

Before moving on from classes, let's explore what inheritance means. This is the processing of reusing code, which is one of the benefits of object-oriented programming. Let's say you're continuing work on your snake project, and you want to organize the reptile into two types: water snakes and land snakes. You know that they share some characteristics, such as being legless and having flicky tongues, but there are also specific characteristics associated with the different snakes. Now, you could create two separate classes, but adding a new common characteristic would mean you have to add it into both of them, and that can quickly become annoying.

What you want to do instead is use the inheritance mechanism. You are creating a type and subtype connection between your classes. Create one class that both water and land snakes can pull - or inherit -

from. Your water and land snakes become sub-types, so when you add your standard features (legless, flicky tongues) to just that parent class, they show up in both sub-types. You are free to add unique and separate features into the sub-types.

Inheritance makes it way easier to keep things organized and to reuse code. You have this base or parent class that sets everything up, and if you need to modify just a piece of it or use its essential functions with some changes, you can refer back to it while creating a new sub-type, and then add (to the sub-type) without messing up the parent class.

Loops

Using loops can also help reduce the amount of code you have to write out every time you want the program to achieve something. Looping is not exclusive to Python; it can be employed in just about every computer language. A loop is a sequence of instructions that keep repeating within the perimeters you set up until the condition you establish is met. It allows you to execute statements or entire groups of comments multiple times without writing out the code each time.

There are two main types of loops in Python: for loops and while loops. For loops run a predetermined number of times, no matter what..

While loops will repeat a single statement or group while the given condition is correct, there is no predetermined number of times for this loop; it's all about true or false. Before beginning the loop, Python tests the condition to confirm whether or not it is true. It will keep executing a block while the state is true, and it will stop if it becomes false.

It is even possible to "nest" a loop, so you're getting a loop within the loop, or an inner loop and an outer loop. Python will cycle through the outer loop, and when it's made a full pass, it triggers the inner loop, which in turn triggers the outer loop again once its run is complete.

You can stop any type of loop by writing break and even skip over a part of code and then begin the loop again by writing continue. Why would you do this? It's advantageous if there are only certain parts of a code you want to use again. Without the option of breaking and continuing the loop, you would have to copy the entire code and then delete the part(s) you didn't want. It's much cleaner to loop. You would usually put your break and continue statement after a certain condition is met. How do you tell Python to be aware of that? You use a conditional if statement.

Conditional statements

Pretty much all programming languages make use of an if statement, which is the main type of conditional statement. It is an essential part of Python's ability to make decisions about running code or not, and if necessary, change a program's flow. The if the statement is similar to a while loop in that it only runs if certain conditions are met, but unlike a while loop, conditionals only run once. Loops make use of conditional statements, but conditional statements do not require loops.

So, you tell Python you want a bit of code only if something is true. To test that, Python uses a Boolean expression, which is just a fancy way of describing a statement that is either true or false. If the answer ends up being false - the conditions are not met - what then? You will use else or elif statements. An else statement just tells the computer what the next step should be, like what block of code it should skip to instead of running the original which doesn't meet the conditions you want.

Elif will commonly appear in the middle of an if statement since it deals with additional conditions, while the else statement often appears at the end and presents a decision.

If you've ever played video games with different dialogue and event options, you've seen conditionals in action. Certain responses are triggered only if you picked the corresponding option, i.e. your character reacts in anger to something that was said instead of calmly, and this triggers a challenge to fight. If you accept, the fight begins, but if you decline, the fight never occurs. If you were to look at the code, you would see a lot of conditionals and instructions to skip over certain code in favour of other blocks, if certain conditions were met.

Exceptions

No code is perfect. When a program is being executed, a problem known as a run-time error can occur. You'll know what these are right away because most error messages will also provide some info about where it happened. When an error occurs, it can cause the entire program to crash, which is why exceptions are so important. Exceptions are virtually signals or flags that let Python know something weird has happened. They disrupt the normal program flow to prevent crashing. Python has built-in limitations that automatically force your program to pause. Here are some of the most common:

IOError
If the file can't be opened

ImportErrorIf Python can't find the module

Handling errors

To handle errors, you set up what is known as exception-handling blocks. Using the keywords/clauses try and except will catch exceptions. Whenever an error occurs inside the try block of code, Python will search for the matching except for block. If found, the program starts running there, preventing a crash. If there is no error, you can program in an else statement, which instructs Python to run whatever block of code you want.

The last keyword to know about: finally. This tells Python what code block it should run no matter what's happened before. Even if there's an error or not, that's the code that should be run last. On the Real Python website, contributor Said van de Klundert breaks this process down in a handy chart:

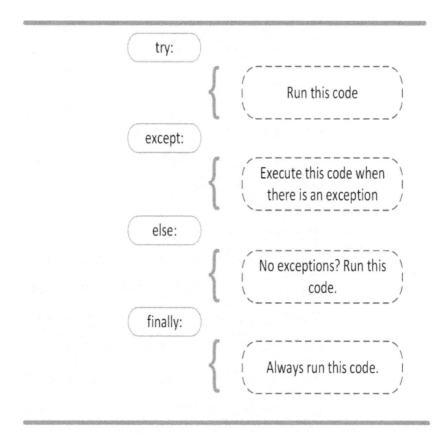

try:

{ Run this code

except:

{ Execute this code when there is an exception

else:

{ No exceptions? Run this code.

finally:

{ Always run this code.

Raising exceptions and assertions

You can also establish and define your exceptions. Why would you purposely do this? Let's say you're working with some code, and you believe it might result in an error. You raise an exception by simply writing raise, which will result in the current execution of the code to break so that the exception can be handled. This is a little different than the try clause, which will only skip to an except clause if an error occurs. Using raise forces the program to skip to the exception right away.

Programmers will also raise exceptions in especially complicated pieces of code that have multiple action options. As soon as the program chooses an option, an exception forces the program to "jump out of the code."

You should also know about making assertions in Python. Whenever Python comes to assert, it will check the expression associated with it and make sure it is true. If it isn't, you can have Python raise an AssertionError exception. When would you use this? Assertions are inserted into code to let programmers know about errors that cannot be fixed in their programs. According to Dan Bader's site, they are purely a debugging tool and not intended for dealing with run-time errors. They let programmers find the original causes of a bug more efficiently. A perfect program would never encounter assertion errors, but no program is perfect.

Other types of errors you might encounter

As you know, exceptions are also called run-time errors. There are two other types of errors that can pop up in a program: syntax and semantic. By knowing the types, you can figure out the solutions more easily. Syntax errors occur when you've forgotten some little thing while typing, like a colon, or added one where it didn't belong. Python will produce a Syntax Error: invalid syntax message so that one is obvious. If you get this message, you'll have to go back over the code and look for mistakes.

Semantic errors are problems that occur while the program is running, but no error messages are produced. For example, you might want a bit of code to run at a certain time, but then it doesn't so that the program won't produce the right result. You won't know that's the reason right away; you have to go back and take a close look at the program's output to figure out what it's doing.

Modules, packages, and libraries

We've talked about inheritance, which allows you to reuse code within a program, but what about codes that will most likely be used for more than one program? You would use modules. These are pieces of software with specific functions. Say you're building a simple checkers game. One module would have all the code for the game's logic, while another one deals with the actual graphics and look of the game on the screen. Each module gets its separate file of code and is edited separately. To bring the whole game together, you import them all into a single program.

Modules can be reused over and over again, and imported from one program to the next. Python has built-in modules which are available from the Python Standard Library. When you open one, you'll see a bunch of code, and if you were to insert it into your program, you would be adding that module's content.

You can also do your modules very simply. Say you've been working on a program and you know you'll want to use part of the code again at some point in another program. Save those lines of code in a file using the file extension .py. Now you're working on your other program and want to import the module you made. Simply use the import statement and the file name. Only want to import part of the module? Use the from the statement, like in this example from w3schools.com: the module is named mymod and contains one function and one dictionary.

```
def greeting(name):

print("Hello, " + name)

person1 = {

    "name": "John",

  "age": 36,

  "country": "Norway"

    }
```

You want to import only the person1 dictionary, so this is what you would type:

```
from mymod import person1
```

Did it work? Check by printing something from the dictionary:

```
print (person1["age"])
```

36

Packages

Packages are just collections of modules. When you've been writing a lot of modules and programs and whatnot, you want to stay as organized as possible. That's what packages are for: they are used to keep relevant modules together in one place. For Python to recognize a package, it should be named as a _init_.py file.

Libraries

Libraries are similar to packages in that they are collections of modules. With libraries, however, they are simply the collections and not a file format. Your search for libraries online based on what sort of program you're working on, so you can use its code and don't have to come up with yours from scratch. We mentioned the Python Standard Library, which is the most famous example of a library. There are hundreds out there that are used for various programming functions. Here are some others that are useful:

Pygame - used for 2d game development

Pyglet - an engine used for 3D animation and game creation

Numby - used for math functions

Pandas - used for data structures and data analysis

Pillow - used for imaging

Twisted - used for networking application development

Requests - an HTTP library

Chapter 3. The Importance of Machine Learning

Why Is Machine Learning So Important?

One topic that we need to spend some time on here is the idea of why machine learning is going to be so important to our world today. There has been a lot of interest from companies in all sorts of industries when it comes to what machine learning is, and it is something that we definitely need to take a look at. Things like the growing amount and the growing types of data, and the idea that we are able to process both of these faster, for less money, and with more accuracy to learn something new out of the data have been big benefits of machine learning, and big reasons why companies want to use this as well.

All of these factors are going to come together and will show us that it is possible to quickly and automatically produce the algorithms and models, with the help of Python, that we need. Today, and in the future, we are going to find that these are the same models that we can use to help analyze the growing and more complex types of data that we are going to find out on, and still provide us with some of the results that we are looking for.

Mainly, many businesses are working with machine learning because they know it is one of the best ways to grow their business. And many of the algorithms that we are able to create when it comes to machine learning and Python working together will ensure that we are able to get some of the best results possible out of this as well. When those two pieces of technology can come together, we will find that it is easier than ever to find patterns and insights into the world of business that we can use in the future as well.

How Does Machine Learning Work?

With this in mind, we also need to take a look at how all of this machine learning is going to work for our needs. Working on algorithms and more with machine learning can seem like a really complex thing to handle, but you will see that a lot of the steps are going to seem easy. To help us get the most out of this process though, we need to make sure that we are not only picking out the right algorithms but that we also come up with the right tools and processes that will get the work done as well.

When you are able to combine together the good data that you have collected, the right tools and processes, and a bit of Python to help run the right algorithm that you want to work with, you will find that machine learning will be able to help your business out more than anything has been able to do in the past. And maybe that is a big reason why machine learning has become so important to so many businesses over time.

Medium and large businesses are able to use data analysis and machine learning to help them reach their customers and stay as successful as possible. But this doesn't mean that they want to sit around and wait forever in order to get that data set up and ready to go. This is why we need to make sure that the tools and processes are paired with the right algorithm are able to keep up with them, and that they will not have to wait around to see the results. This doesn't mean that machine learning is going to be an instant solution and that it doesn't take some time. but we need to make sure that it all fits together and that we are able to get some good results out of it without having to wait months or years to get it done.

So, the first thing that we need to have in order to get machine learning to do the work that we would like is the right algorithm. Most of these algorithms are going to run thanks to the Python coding language, which makes them one of the perfect ways to handle all of that data. But you will quickly find that when you are working with data analysis and all of the parts that need to come with this, you will find that there are a lot of different algorithms that we are able to pick from.

Keep in mind wit this one that there are a ton of algorithms that you are able to choose from, and the one that you choose for your needs is going to depend on the data that you have collected, the kind of questions that you want to ask along the way, and what you are hoping to find out when the process is done.

The variety of algorithms can be great though because it helps us to make sure that we are able to find the one that works the best for our needs. There are many choices though including random forests, neural networks, clustering, decision trees, support vector machines, and so much more.

While we are here though, we need to also make sure that we are using the right tools along with the algorithms in order to handle the data and provide us with the insights and data that we are looking for along the way. this is important because it ensures the algorithm is actually able to handle the data that we want. Some of the tools that are available for programmers to choose when it is time to work on a data analysis along the way will include:

1.   A comprehensive amount of management for our data, and high-quality data.

2.   GUIS to help us to build up the models that we want to use with machine learning. And a good process flow.

3.   A way to compare some of the different models that come with machine learning so we have a better chance of figuring out which one is the best for our needs.

4.   Interactive exploration of any data that we want to handle so that it is easier to see what small changes are going to do with our information and also a visualization of our model results.

5.   Automated ensemble model to make it easier to identify some of the performers who are doing the best.

6.   A platform that is integrated to handle some of the automation that we need in our data, speeding up the process that we need for the data to decision selection.

7.   A model deployment system that is easy so that we are able to get results quickly that are reliable and repeatable.

As we are able to see here, the algorithms that we want to use for our data analysis are going to be important, but it is even more critical to our process if we are able to take those algorithms and combine them with the right tools to get the work done. Having these together, and ensuring that they are compatible and going to work for the data that we have will make a difference in whether or not you are going to be able to use that data to make some smart business decisions along the way.

Chapter 4. Types of Learning Machines

Types of Learning

Machine learning is a type of automated learning that has little to no intervention by humans. The purpose is to explore data and to construct algorithms that can learn from old data and make predictions on new data. The input data is training data, and this is what represents the experience; the output is the expertise, usually a separate algorithm that performs some task. Input data can be in many formats – text, numerical, visual, audio, or multimedia. The output that corresponds to the input can be afloat (a floating-point number), an integer or an image of some description.

The Learning Concepts
Machine learning is the process of taking experience and turning it into knowledge or expertise. We can classify learning into three broad categories, each based on the learning data nature and the interaction between the environment and the learner:

- Supervised Learning

- Unsupervised Learning

- Semi-supervised Learning

In the same way, machine algorithms can also be categorized in four directions:

- Supervised learning algorithm

- Unsupervised learning algorithm

- Semi-supervised learning algorithm

- Reinforcement learning algorithm

Supervised and unsupervised are the two most common ones, and they are the ones we will discuss now.

Supervised Learning

Supervised learning is the commonly used method for real-world applications, like speech or facial recognition, sales forecasts and more. We can classify supervised learning as two distinct types – regression and classification.

- Regression trains on data and predicts responses that are of a continuous value type, like the prediction of real-estate prices.

- Classification tries to find the right class label, for example, analysis of positive or negative sentiment, the distinction between male and female, between malignant and benign tumours, unsecured or secured loans, and so on.

With supervised learning, all the data is complete with a description, a label, the targets or the output desired; the goal of it is to find the generalized rule that will map the inputs to the outputs. We call this kind of data labelled data, and the control that has been learned is then used to mark the new data with unknown productions.

Supervised learning is building a model that is based on data samples with labels. For example, if we wanted a system that estimated house or land prices based on certain features, we would need to create the database with the elements in it and then label it. The algorithm needs to be taught what features correspond to which prices and, based on the data it gets, it learns how to make the price calculation using the input features values.

With supervised learning, we are dealing with a computer system that takes available training data and learns a function from it. The algorithm analyzes the data producing a feature that can then be used for new examples. Types of supervised learning algorithms include neural networks, logistic regression, Naïve Bayes, and support vector machines. In contrast, common supervised learning examples include labelling web pages as per the content they have, voice recognition, facial recognition, and learning to classify an email as spam or not spam.

Unsupervised Learning

We use unsupervised learning to detect oddities, to put customers with like behaviours together in groups for sales campaigns, detect outliers like defective equipment or fraud, and so on. It is the complete opposite of supervised learning, and none of the data is labelled.

When the training data have no labels and no descriptions, and just a few indications, it is down to the coder or down to the algorithm to work out what the structure is to the underlying data. The algorithm needs to find the patterns hidden in the data or work out how the data should be described. We call this data unlabeled.

Let's assume that we have several data points, and we want them classified into several groups. At this stage, we probably don't know what the classification criterion is, so the unsupervised algorithm will attempt to organize the data into a given number of groups using the optimum way.

These are incredibly powerful algorithms for the analysis of data and for finding any trends or patterns in that data. They are used mostly for clustering similar inputs into groups in a logical way. Some of the standard unsupervised algorithms include hierarchical clustering, random forests, and K-Means, among others.

Semi-supervised Learning

If we have a dataset with some labelled and some unlabeled data, we call it semi-supervised learning. This algorithm uses the unlabeled data to train on and the labelled data to test on. It tends to be used where it is too expensive in computational terms to get a dataset that is fully labelled while labelling a smaller subset is a good deal more practical. For example, we sometimes need experts who are highly skilled to mark some images, perhaps remote sensing images, and a lot of field experiments to find oil in a specific place; the acquisition of unlabeled data is quite easy by comparison.

Reinforcement Learning

With reinforcement learning, the data will provide feedback so that the system can adjust itself dynamically to achieve a specific objective. The system will evaluate its performance based on that feedback, and it will react accordingly. Some of the best-known uses for reinforcement learning are AlphaGo, which we mentioned earlier and the self-drive cars.

Applications of Machine Learning Algorithms

Machine learning algorithms are used in many different forms, such as:

- Data mining

- Expert systems

- Forecasting such as stock market trends, weather

- Games

- Language processing

- Pattern recognition

- Robotics

- Vision processing

Steps Involved in Machine Learning

A machine learning project will involve these steps:

- Definition of a Problem

- Preparation of the Data

- Evaluation of the Algorithms

- Improving the Results

- Presentation of the Results

The very best way to understand machine learning is to follow a Python project from start to finish and cover the most important steps:

- Load the data

- Summarize the data

- Evaluate the algorithms

- Make predictions

This will produce a method that is replicable, which means it can be used on multiple datasets. Extra data can be added to improve the results even further.

Setting Up the Environment

Although we covered installing Python earlier, we need to look into how to install the required packages and libraries.

Installation

Installing Python can be done in two ways – the method we looked at earlier was installing directly from the Python website, or you can install a Python distribution called Anaconda. With the first method, once you have installed Python, use the following commands to install the packages:

$pip install NumPy

$pip install matplotlib

$pip install pandas

$pip install seaborn

The second method, using Anaconda includes Jupyter Notebook already built-in – this is an interactive environment for Python – and it also consists of the packages that you need already integrated. We download Anaconda from Continuum Analytics – it will take up to 20 minutes to do as Anaconda contains Python, the packages, a built-in code editor, and other files.

Now you can open Anaconda Navigator and go into Spyder IDE or Jupyter. Once you are in, type the following commands to import the packages:

import NumPy

import matplotlib

Next, check to see if the installation has been successful by typing this command at the command line:

$ python

Python 3.6.3 |Anaconda custom (32-bit)| (default, 'system data and time')

[GCC 7.2.0] on (operating system)

The required libraries can be imported, and their versions printed:

>>>import numpy

>>>print numpy.__version__

x.xx.xx(version number)

>>> import matplotlib

>>> print (matplotlib.__version__)

x.x.x(version)

```
>> import pandas

>>> print (pandas.__version__)

x.xx.x(version)

>>> import seaborn

>>> print (seaborn.__version__)

x.x.x(version number)
```

The Purpose of Machine Learning

We know that machine learning is a subset of Artificial Intelligence (AI) because the ability to take experience and turn into expertise or to see a pattern in a bunch of complex data is human or animal-level intelligence. As a science field, machine learning shares several concepts with disciplines, such as information theory, statistics, optimization, and game theory. Its objective as an IT subfield is to program a machine so that it can learn.

However, it must be realized that machine learning is not just about building a duplication of human or animal intelligent behaviour. Machine learning can also be used for the detection of patterns that are way beyond the scope of both animal and human perception.

Chapter 5. Data Processing with Machine Learning

Several Examples of Data Processing with Machine Learning:

Machine Learning Algorithms

By utilizing prior computations and underlying algorithms, machines are now capable of learning from and training on their own to generate high quality, readily reproducible decisions and results. The notion of machine learning has been around for a long time now, but the latest advances in machine learning algorithms have made extensive data processing and analysis feasible for computers. This is achieved by applying sophisticated and complicated mathematical calculations using high speed and frequency automation. Today's advanced computing machines are able to analyze humongous information quantities quickly and deliver quicker and more precise outcomes. Companies using machine learning algorithms have increased flexibility to change the training data set to satisfy their company needs and train the machines accordingly. These tailored algorithms of machine learning enable companies to define potential hazards and possibilities for development. Typically, machine learning algorithms are used in cooperation with artificial intelligence technology and cognitive techniques to create computers extraordinarily efficient and extremely effective in exact outcomes.

There are four fundamental types of machine learning algorithms available today:

Supervised Machine Learning Algorithms

Due to their ability to evaluate and apply the lessons learned from prior iterations and interactions to raw input data set, the supervised learning algorithms are commonly used in predictive big data analysis. Based on the instructions given to predict and forecast future occurrences effectively, these algorithms can label all their ongoing runs. For instance, people can program the machine as "R" (Run), "N" (Negative) or "P" (Positive) to label its data points. The algorithm for machine learning will then mark the input data as programmed and obtain data inputs with the right outputs. The algorithm will compare its own produced production to the "anticipated or correct" output, identifying future changes that can be created and fixing mistakes to make the model more precise and smarter. By using methods such as "regression," "prediction," "classification" and "ingredient boosting" to train the machine learning algorithms well, any new input data can be fed into the machine as a set of "target" data to orchestrate the learning program as desired. This "known training data set" jump-starts the analytical process followed by the learning algorithm to produce an "inferred feature" that can be used to generate forecasts and predictions based on output values for future occurrences. For instance, financial institutions and banks rely strongly on monitoring machine learning algorithms to detect credit card fraud and predict the probability of a prospective credit card client failing to make their credit payments on time.

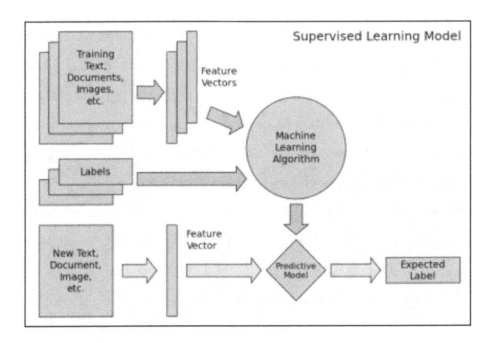

Unsupervised Machine Learning Algorithms

Companies often find themselves in a scenario where information sources are inaccessible that are needed to produce a labelled and classified training data set. Using unsupervised ML algorithms is perfect in these circumstances. Unsupervised ML algorithms are widely used to define how the machine can generate "inferred features" to elucidate a concealed construct from the stack of unlabeled and unclassified data collection. These algorithms can explore the data in order to define a structure within the data mass. Unlike the supervised machine learning algorithms, the unsupervised algorithms fail to identify the correct output, although they are just as effective as the supervised learning algorithms in investigating input data and drawing inferences. These algorithms can be used to identify information outliers, generate tailored and custom product recommendations, classify text subjects using methods such as "self-organizing maps," "singular value decomposition" and "k-means clustering." For instance, customer identification with shared shopping characteristics that can be segmented into particular groups and focused on comparable marketing strategies and campaigns. As a result, in the online marketing world, unsupervised learning algorithms are prevalent.

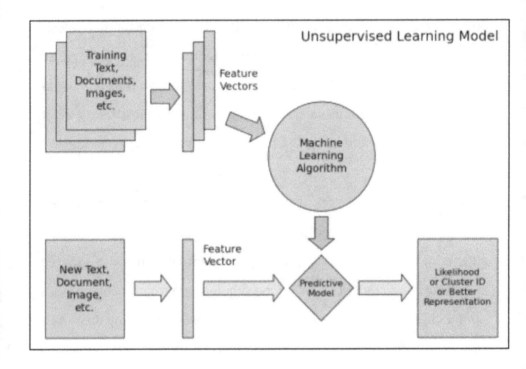

Semi-Supervised Machine Learning Algorithms

Highly versatile, the "semi-supervised machine learning algorithms" are capable of using both labelled and unlabeled information set to learn from and train themselves. These algorithms are a "hybrid" of algorithms that are supervised and unsupervised. Typically, with a small volume of labelled data, the training data set is comprised of predominantly unlabeled data. The use of analytical methods, including "forecast," "regression" and "classification" in conjunction with semi-supervised learning algorithms enable the machine to enhance its learning precision and training capabilities considerably. These algorithms are commonly used in instances where it is highly resource-intensive and less cost-effective for the business to generate labelled training data set from raw unlabeled data. Companies use semi-supervised learning algorithms on their systems to avoid incurring extra costs of staff and equipment. For instance, the implementation of "facial recognition" technology needs a considerable amount of facial data distributed across various sources of input. The raw data pre-processing, processing, classification and labelling, acquired from sources such as internet cameras, needs a lot of resources and thousands of hours of the job to be used as a training data set.

Reinforcement Machine Learning Algorithms

The "reinforcement machine learning algorithms" are much more distinctive in that they learn from the environment. These algorithms conduct activities and record the outcomes of each action diligently, which would have been either a failure resulting in mistake or reward for an excellent performance. The two primary features that differentiate the reinforcement learning algorithms are the research method of "trial and error" and feedback loop of "delayed reward." The computer continually analyzes input data and sends a reinforcement signal for each right or anticipated output to ultimately optimize the end result. The algorithm develops a straightforward action and reward feedback loop to evaluate record and learn which activities have been practical and in a shorter period have resulted in correct or expected output. The use of these algorithms allows the system to automatically determine optimal behaviors and maximize its efficiency within the constraints of a particular context. The reinforcement machine learning algorithms are therefore actively used in gaming, robotics engineering and navigation systems.

The machine learning algorithms have proliferated to hundreds and thousands and counting. Here are some of the most widely used algorithms:

1. Regression

The "regression" techniques fall under the category of supervised machine learning. They help predict or describe a particular numerical value based on the set of prior information, such as anticipating the cost of a property based on previous cost information for similar characteristics. Regression techniques vary from simple (such as "linear regression") to complex (such as "regular linear regression," "polynomial regression," "decision trees," "random forest regression" and "neural networks," among others).

The simplest method of all is "linear regression," where the line's "mathematical equation $(y= m*x+b)$ is used to model the data collection." Multiple "data pairs (x, y)" can train a "linear regression" model by calculating the position and slope of a line that can decrease the total distance between the data points and the track. In other words, the calculation of the "slope (m)" and "y-intercept (b)" is used for a line that produces the highest approximation for data observations.

For example, using "linear regression" technique to generate predictions for the energy consumption (in kWh) of houses by collecting the age of the house, no. of bedrooms, square footage area and the number of installed electronic equipment. Now, we have more than one input (year built, square footage) it is possible to use "linear multi-variable regression." The underlying process is the same as "one-to-one linear regression"; however, the line created was based on the number of variables in multi-dimensional space.

The plot below demonstrates how well the model of linear regression fits the real construction energy consumption. In a case where you could gather house characteristics such as year built and square footage, but you do not understand the house's energy consumption then you are better off using the fitted line to generate approximations for the house's energy consumption.

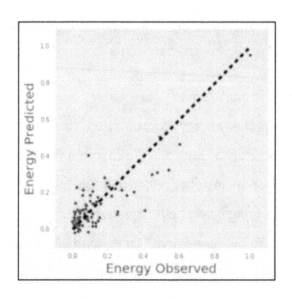

"Multiple Linear Regression" tends to be the most common form of "regression" technique used in data science and the majority of statistical tasks. Just like the "linear regression" technique, there will be an output variable "Y" in "multiple linear regression." However, the distinction now is that we are going to have numerous "X" or independent variables generating predictions for "Y."

For instance, a model developed for predicting the cost of housing in Washington DC will be driven by "multiple linear regression" technique. The cost of housing in Washington DC will be the "Y" or dependent variable for the model. "X" or the independent variables for this model will include data points such as vicinity to public transport, schooling district, square footage, number of rooms, which will eventually determine the market price of the housing.

The mathematical equation for this model can be written as below:

"housing_price = $\beta 0$ + $\beta 1$ sq_foot + $\beta 2$ dist_transport + $\beta 3$ num_rooms"

"Polynomial regression" - Our models developed a straight line in the last two types of "regression" techniques. This straight line is a result of the connection between "X" and "Y" which is "linear" and does not alter the influence "X" has on "Y" as the changing values of "X." Our model will lead in a row with a curve in "polynomial regression."

If we attempted to fit a graph with non-linear features using "linear regression," it would not yield the best fit line for the non-linear features. For instance, the graph on the left shown in the picture below has the scatter plot depicting an upward trend, but with a curve. A straight line does not operate in this situation. Instead, we will generate a line with a curve to match the curve in our data with a polynomial regression, like the chart on the right shown in the picture below. The equation of a polynomial will appear like the linear equation, the distinction being that one or more of the "X" variables will be linked to some polynomial expression. For instance,

"$Y = mX2+b$"

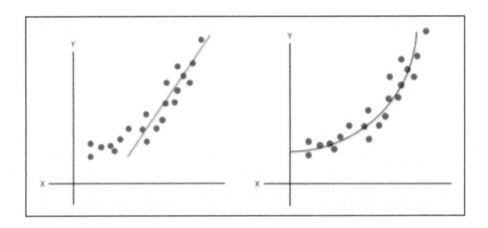

Another technique of reduction is called "LASSO regression." A very complementary method to the "ridge regression," "lasso regression" promotes the use of simpler and leaner models to generate predictions. In lasso regression, the model reduces the value of coefficients relatively more rigidly. LASSO stands for the "least absolute shrinkage and selection operator." Data on our scatterplot, like the mean or median values of the data are reduced to a more compact level. We use this when the model is experiencing high multicollinearity similar to the "ridge regression" model.

A hybrid of "LASSO" and "ridge regression" methods is known as "ElasticNet Regression." Its primary objective is to enhance further the accuracy of the predictions generated by the "LASSO regression" technique. "ElasticNet Regression" is a confluence of both "LASSO" and "ridge regression" techniques of rewarding smaller coefficient values. All three of these designs are available in the R and Python "Glmnet suite."

"Bayesian regression" models are useful when there is a lack of sufficient data, or available data has poor distribution. These regression models are developed based on probability distributions rather than data points, meaning the resulting chart will appear as a bell curve depicting the variance with the most frequently occurring values in the centre of the curve. The dependent variable "Y" in "Bayesian regression" is not a valuation but a probability. Instead of predicting a value, we try to estimate the likelihood of an occurrence. This is regarded as "frequentist statistics," and this sort of statistics is built on the "Bayes theorem." "Frequentist statistics" hypothesize if an event is going to occur and the probability of it happening again in the future.

"Conditional probability" is integral to the concept of "frequentist statistics." Conditional probability pertains to the events whose results are dependent on one another. Events can also be contingent, which means the other event can potentially alter the likelihood of the next event. Assume you have a box of M&Ms, and you want to understand the probability of withdrawing distinct colors of the M&Ms from the bag. If you have a set of three yellow M&Ms and three blue M&Ms and on your first draw you get a blue M&M, and then with your next draw from the box the probability of taking out a blue M&M will be lower than the first draw. This is a classic example of "conditional probability." On the other hand, an independent event is the flipping of a coin, meaning the front coin flip does not alter the probability of the next flip of the coin. Therefore, a coin flip is not an example of "conditional probability."

2. Classification

The method of "classification" is another class of "supervised machine learning," which can generate predictions or explanations for a "class value." For example, this method can be used to predict if an online customer will actually purchase a particular product. The result generated will be reported as a yes or no response, i.e. "buyer" or "not a buyer." However, techniques of classification are not restricted to two classes. A classification technique, for instance, could assist in evaluating whether a specified picture includes a sedan or an SUV. The output will be three different values in this case: 1) the picture contains a sedan, 2) the picture contains an SUV, or 3) the picture does not contain either a sedan or an SUV.

"Logistic regression" is considered the easiest classification algorithm, though the term comes across as a "regression" technique, but that is far from reality. "Logistic regression" generates estimations for the likelihood of an event taking place based on single or multiple input values. For example, to generate estimation for the likelihood of a student being accepted to a specific university, a "logistic regression" will use the standardized testing scores and university testing scores for a student as inputs. The generated prediction is a probability, ranging between '0' and '1,' where 1 is full assurance. For the student, if the estimated likelihood is greater than 0.5, then the prediction would be that they will be accepted. If the projected probability were less than 0.5, the prediction would be that they would be denied admission.

The following graph shows the ratings of past learners as well as whether they have been accepted. Logistic regression enables the creation of a line that can represent the "decision boundary."

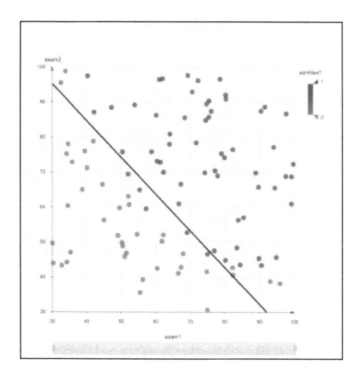

3. Clustering

We enter the category of unsupervised machine learning, with "clustering methods" because its objective is to "group or cluster observations with comparable features." Clustering methods do not use output data to train but allow the output to be defined by the algorithm. Only data visualizations can be used in clustering techniques to check the solution's quality.

"K-Means clustering," where 'K' is used to represent the number of "clusters" that the customer elects to generate and is the most common clustering method. (Note that different methods for selecting K value, such as the "elbow technique," are available.)

Steps used by K-Means clustering to process the data points:

1. The data centers are selected randomly by 'K.'

2. Assigns each data point to the nearest centers that have been randomly generated.

3. Re-calculates each cluster's center.

4. If centers do not change (or have minor change), the process will be completed.

- Otherwise, we will go back to step two. (Set a maximum amount of iterations in advance to avoid being stuck in an infinite loop, if the center of the cluster continues to alter.)

The following plot applies "K-Means" to a building data set. Each column in the plot shows each building's efficiency. The four measurements relate to air conditioning, heating, installed electronic appliances (refrigerators, TV) and cooking gas. For simplicity of interpretation of the results, 'K' can be set to value '2' for clustering, wherein one cluster will be selected as an efficient building group and the other cluster as an inefficient building group. You see the place of the structures on the left as well as a couple of the building characteristics used as inputs on the right: installed electronic appliances and heating.

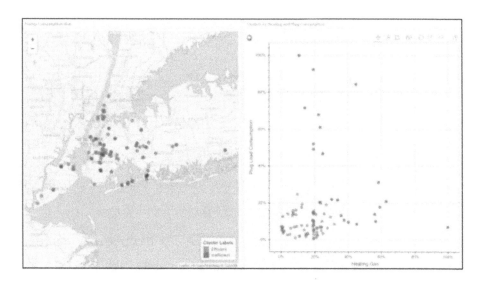

4. Dimension Reduction

As the name indicates, to extract the least significant information (sometimes redundant columns) from a data set, we use "dimensionality reduction." In practice, data sets tend to contain hundreds or even thousands of rows (also known as characteristics), which makes it essential to reduce the total number of rows. For example, pictures may contain thousands of pixels; not all those pixels are important for the analysis. Alternatively, a large number of measurements or experiments can be applied to every single chip while testing microchips within the manufacturing process, the majority of which produce redundant data. In such scenarios, "dimensionality reduction" algorithms are leveraged to manage the data set.

Principal Component Analysis

"Principal Component Analysis" or (PCA) is the most common "dimension reduction technique," which decreases the size of the "feature space" by discovering new vectors that are capable of maximizing the linear variety of the data. When the linear correlations of the data are powerful, PCA can dramatically decrease the data dimension without losing too much information. PCA is one of the fundamental algorithms of machine learning. It enables you to decrease the data dimension, losing as little information as possible.

It is used in many fields such as object recognition, the vision of computers, compression of information, etc. The calculation of the main parts is limited to the calculation of the initial data's own vectors and covariance matrix values or to the data matrix's unique decomposition. Through one, we can convey several indications, merge, so to speak, and operate with a simpler model already. Of course, most probably, data loss will not be avoided, but the PCA technique will assist us to minimize any losses.

Chapter 6. Data Science Basics Process

Why Is Data Science So Important?

To start with, we need to figure out why this data science industry is so important. In a world that is turning more to the digital space than it ever did before, organizations are going to deal with a ton of data, data that is unstructured and structured, daily. Some of the evolving technologies that we can look at have enabled us to save a lot of money, and smart storage spaces have come up to store a lot of this data until companies can get to it.

Currently, there is a huge need for skilled and certified data scientists to help go through this information and see what is found inside. When it comes to the IT industry, these data scientists are going to be among the highest-paid professionals out there. In fact, According to Forbes, the annual salary for the average data scientist is almost $110,000.

Why is this industry paying so much? Because it is in high demand and many companies are looking to find qualified professionals who can gather, store, and look through all of the data that they have available. And provide them with predictions, information, and help in using this information to make sound business decisions. And the number of professionals who can process and derive valuable insights out of the data are few and far between, so they are in high demand.

There are going to be some requirements that have to come into play so that someone who handles this data because of all of these issues, there is actually about a 50 per cent gap in the industry when it comes to the demand for a data scientist versus how many of these professionals who are out there. This is another reason why it is so essential for us to learn a bit more about the world of data science and how this is going to be a topic that many businesses will want to work with as well.

When we keep this in mind, it is still essential for many companies to focus a bit more on the beauty of data science and some of the different steps that we are going to need to focus on as well. As we go through this book, you will find that there are quite a few steps that we need to follow to see some success with data science along the way, which is why it usually takes a professional to go through and handle all of this.

And this is the same information that companies are going to try and use to get ahead and learn more than their competitors. And, likely, this growth of data is not going to die out any time soon, which means that we are going to see more and more data that a company can use.

Right now, each day we are going to see 25 quintillion bytes of data generated for companies to use, and it is going to grow at an even faster rate as IoT continues to grow this is an extraordinary amount of growth in data. Which can be useful for a lot of companies to learn about their customers, figure out the best products to release next, and work the best with the customer service they would like to provide. All of this data is going to come from a variety of sources that will include:

1. Sensors are set up in shopping malls to gather up the information of the individual shopper.

2.   Posts on the various platforms of social media can send back information to the company.

3.   Videos that are found on our phones and digital pictures are taking in more data than ever before.

4. Companies are able even to get some good information when they look at some of the purchase transactions that come when people shop online and through e-commerce.

All of these different data, no matter where we are going to see it from, is going to be called big data. As you can imagine here from all of the various sources of data and what we have talked about so far in this topic, companies are going to search for data, and find that they are flooded with more data than they know what to do within the first place. It is a ton of data, and assuming that one person, or even a small group of people, can go through it manually and effectively is pretty much foolish.

They will take too long, miss out on things, or misread these things, and by the time they came up with the insights, especially with how fast the world of data is being created, the ideas and predictions are going to be old.

This is why data science is going to be so essential for us to focus our attention on. We will find that when we work with this data science, we are going to be able to learn better what we can do with all of this data, and some of the best ways that we can utilize this data to make some right decisions about our business in the future.

It is here that the idea of data science is going to start showing up into the picture. Data science is going to bring together a ton of skills that we can find in the world of business, including business domain knowledge, mathematics, and statistics. All of these are important because they are going to help an organization out in a variety of ways, including:

1. Helping the company learn new techniques where they can reduce costs each day.

2. It can improve the company to figure out the best method to take to get into a new market that will be profitable for them.

3.   This can help the company learn about a variety of demographics and how to tap into these

4. It can improve the company to take a look at the marketing campaign that they sent out there and then figure out if the marketing campaign was useful.

5. It can make it easier for the company to launch a new service product successfully.

These are just a few of the things that this big data is going to be able to help us out. This means that no matter what kind of industry will be able to use the ideas of data science to help them learn about their customers, their marketing campaigns, their products, and more and lead up to more success for the company.

As a business owner, you will find that there are a ton of ways that we can work with data science to help us out. Let's explore some of the different things that we are able to do to handle our data science project, no matter what kind of company we are in the first place.

Chapter 7. How Machine Learning Works For Data Science

When we are talking about data science and some of the different processes that come with it, you will find that we can't get very far in this process without learning a bit more about machine learning and all of the different parts that come with that as well. All of the algorithms that we are going to talk about with data science will rely on machine learning to help them happen.

Machine learning is going to be one of the many branches that we are going to see when we talk about artificial intelligence. This means that it is going to be one of the types of artificial intelligence, but it is not the same, and it is not going to encompass all of the parts of artificial intelligence can do as well. This branch is going to be used and based on the idea that a system can learn from the data it is going to be presented with, it can identify patterns, and it can make some smart decisions based on the data.

Because of all of the different technologies that are out there to help us with computing and more, machine learning that we rely on today is going to be a bit different than how it was in the beginning. It was initially born from the idea of recognizing patterns, and the idea that a computer and some of the other systems can learn on their own, without needing to have a programmer who would tell it what to do with every step.

Think about how amazing this can be! We can teach the computer how to handle a lot of different tasks, all on its own. We can train it and test it and then have the system go through the process that is necessary to figure things out without us having to individually go through and explain all of the steps to it or program it this way, either. This is something that may have seemed impossible in the past, but it is something that we can do now with some of our modern technology.

While many of the algorithms that work with machine learning have been around us for several years now. Some changes have made it even more fun to learn about today. The ability for this kind of learning to automatically apply mathematical calculations that are complex too big data (which is what we need it to do when we work in data science), over and over while getting faster in the process, is a more recent development. There are a lot of different ways that this machine learning can already be used, and that we already see it used in our daily lives, and these include:

1. The self-driving Google car is one of the most prominent examples right now of machine learning at work.

2.   Any of the online recommendations offers that we see on various websites as we shop.

3. Machine learning can work with something known as linguistic rule creation to help companies understand what customers and others are saying on Twitter and other social media accounts.

4.   Fraud detection has been in use with financial institutions for some time now, and when it is powered by machine learning, we are going to see some great results.

All of the new interest that has come with machine learning is due to some of the same factors that have made data mining, and other parts of data science, so important in our modern world. Things like the growing amount and the different types of data that companies can get their hands on have helped to raise some of the interest. Add in that the processing power for doing the computations is cheaper and more potent than ever before, and that companies are finding new and innovative ways to store the data. And it is no wonder that machine learning and artificial intelligence are two parts of data science that are growing.

When we keep this in mind, we have to remember that there are a few things that we must get in place in order to create a system of machine learning that is actually good. We need to make sure, to start with, that the system we are working with has some capabilities to do preparation of the data. We need a combination of more advanced algorithms, and some basic ones, to help go through the data. We need to have some scalability that shows up, too, because we need to make sure that the program can handle a large amount of data as well. And then, we need to work with something that is known as ensemble modelling.

Before we move on with this, there are a few other parts that are going to come with this machine learning process that we need to focus on, as well. To start, when we work with this machine learning, the target is going to be known as a label. But in statistics, we are going to call this the dependent variable instead. And the variable that we talk about in statistics is going to be a feature when we go back into the machine learning algorithm and use statistics for that algorithm as well.

Chapter 8. Numbers, Functions, and Operators

Numbers

Let's talk about numbers first. This data type stores numeric values, as the name indicates. There's nothing mysterious there. Four numerical examples are supported: integers, long integers, floating-point real values, and complex numbers. As you read other resources about Python and get into more intense learning, you'll see these types often abbreviated as int, long, float, and complex. Don't worry about what those mean exactly; all you have to know is that Python supports different types of numbers.

Functions and modules in python

In Python programming, functions refer to any group of related statements which perform a given activity. Functions are used in breaking down programs into smaller and modular bits. In that sense, functions are the key factors which make programs easier to manage and organize as they grow bigger over time. Functions are also helpful in avoiding repetition during coding and makes codes reusable.

• The Syntax of Functions:

The syntax of functions refers to the rules which govern the combination of characters that make up a function. These syntaxes include the following:

1.   The keyword "def" highlights the beginning of every function header.

2.   A function named is to identify it distinctly. The rules of making functions are the same as the rules which apply for writing identifiers in Python.

3.   Parameters or arguments via which values are passed onto a function are optional in Python.

4.   A colon sign (:) is used to highlight the end of every function header.

5. The optional documentation string known as doing string is used to define the purpose of the function.

6.   The body of a function is comprised of one or more valid statements in Python. The statements must all have a similar indentation level, (typically four spaces).

7.   An optional return statement is included for returning a value from a function.

Below is a representation of the essential components of a function as described in the syntax.

def function_name(parameters):

'''docstring'''

statement(s)

- How functions are called in Python:

Once a function has been defined in Python, it is capable of being called from another function. A program, or the python prompt even. Calling a function is done by entering a function name with a proper parameter.

1.   Docstring:

The docstring is the first string which comes after the function header. The docstring is short for documentation string and is used in explaining what a function does briefly. Although it is an optional part of a function, the documentation process is a good practice in programming. So, unless you have got an excellent memory which can recall what you had for breakfast on your first birthday, you should document your code at all times. In the example shown below, the docstring is used directly beneath the function header.

>>> greet("Amos")

Hello, Amos. Good morning!

Triple quotation marks are typically used when writing docstrings so they can extend to several lines. Such a string is inputted as the __doc__ attribute of the function. Take the example below.

You can run the following lines of code in a Python shell and see what it outputs:

```
1. >>> print(greet.__doc__)
2. This function greets to
3.          the person passed into the
4.          name parameter
```

2.   The return statement:

The purpose is to go back to the location from which it was called after exiting a function.

• Syntax of return:

This statement can hold expressions which have been evaluated and have their values returned. A function will return the Noneobject if the statement is without an expression, or its return statement is itself   absent   in   the   function.   For   instance:

```
1. >>> print(greet('Amos'))
2. Hello, Amos. Good morning!
3. None
```

In this case, the returned value is None.

Adding More Features and Functions

Were we to stop there, we would already have a relatively decent little game to play, and we would have learned a few useful lessons.

But it's by pushing onward and honing and refining our game that we'll be able to learn even more advanced skills!

There's still a little bit of basic tidying up to do.

The first thing we need to do, is to prevent our user from entering too many characters at once. That's easy enough to do using code that we've used a few times at this point:

```python
while Lives > 0:

    print(DrawSpaces(Word, ReferenceWord), "\n")

    if "_" not in DrawSpaces(Word, ReferenceWord):

        Winner = 1

        break

    print("Lives: ", Lives, "\n", "\n")

    LetterGuess = input("Guess a letter: ")

    if len(LetterGuess) > 1:

        print("Enter one character at a time! \n")

    else:
```

```
Lives = Lives - 1

if LetterGuess in Word:

    print("Got one!")

    ReferenceWord = ReferenceWord + LetterGuess

else:

    print("Nope!")
```

Reading From Files

While our hangman game is quite elegant in the way that the code has been written, it is still somewhat limited. Adding new words in those quotation marks will take a lot of time, and with the best will in the world, you're probably not going to sit there and write thousands of words.

Wouldn't it be better if we could play the game in such a way that we could reference an external file? That way, our players might even be able to add more words themselves. We could also have different categories of words and get the players to choose from them themselves!

This is something we can do fairly quickly, and the best part is that we don't even need to reference an additional library – the functionality is built right into the core of Python.

So to do what you want to do, use the following code:

```
from random import randint

with open('D:/words.txt') as f:

    Lines = f.read().splitlines()

Word = Lines[randint(0,len(Lines) -1)]

ReferenceWord = ""
```

What we have done here is to open the file 'words.txt' from the D:\ drive and then split it into a list called 'Lines'. We could also write lines this way and do all manner of other useful things!

All you need to do is to make your text file and fill it with words that you want to include in your game!

Now when you play the game, it will randomly pick one line from the text file, and you can keep adding to these as you go.

Operators

You've seen us use symbols like = and + in our term explanations so far, and in programming, those have names: operators. They come from logic and mathematics and serve to manipulate values through every part of a program, whether it's simple counting or sophisticated security encryption. There are a variety of operators that can manage the code, such as your primary = symbol, which is an assignment operator. And your arithmetic operators, like +, -, *, /, and so on.

There are others, like the Boolean operators or logical operators, and relational operators. Boolean operators include "And," "AndAloso," "OrElse," "Or," "Not," and "Xor." Relationship operators are evaluated variables and compare or contrast to one another. These appear as the greater than symbol, lesser than, and so on. If these last two are a bit confusing, don't stress about it right now. They make more sense in practice.

Chapter 9.   Tips And Tricks For An Intermediate Python Programmer

Code everyday

Practice makes perfect. When learning a new language like Chinese or Spanish, experts recommend you use it every day in the form of speaking and going through an exercise or so. It's no different from a programming language. The more you practice, the more the basic syntax will become second nature to you, and you'll instinctively know when to use concepts like conditionals and loops. There are lots of resources that provide exercises and sample programs you can work on right away.

Write by hand

When you're taking notes (and you should take notes), write them out by hand. Studies show that the process of choosing a physical pen to physical paper facilitates the best long-term memory retention. Writing by hand includes writing code by hand, and then checking it on your computer, so you know for sure if it's accurate. Outlining code and ideas this way can help you stay organized, as well, before starting actually to build a program.

Find other beginners

Learning to code by yourself can get tedious and frustrating. One of the best ways to learn and improve is to find others who are in the same phase as you. You can bounce ideas off each other, help out on projects, and more. If you don't know anyone in your immediate circle, you can check out groups online and find local events through Meetups and Facebook. Always exercise caution and employ safe practices when first meeting people you only know online. Stick to public places during daylight hours, and don't go anywhere alone with someone you don't know well until you feel comfortable.

Try explaining Python out loud.

Sometimes explaining something you just learned to someone is the best way to cement it into your mind. It allows you to reframe concepts into your own words. You don't even have to talk to a real person; it can be an inanimate object. This is such a common practice among programmers that it's known as "rubber duck debugging," which references talking to a rubber duck about bugs in a program. Pick a topic in Python like conditionals or variables, and see if you can explain it. If you have trouble or realize there's a gap in your knowledge, it's time to go back and keep learning.

Check out other languages.

This book is about Python, so obviously we believe that should be your priority, but getting to know a little bit about other languages can be very helpful, too. It will make you a better programmer in the future. Checking out other languages can help you discover what typical architecture is built into every language as well as the differences between them and Python. Even if you just read about other languages and never write much code in anything besides Python, you'll be improving your knowledge and skill.

Have a plan for when you get stuck

When you get stuck while coding, take a step back, what are you trying to get the code to do? What have you tried? And what's happening? Write the answers down and be as specific and detailed as possible. Then, you can go to someone else for help, and you won't have to spend a ton of time trying to explain the problem. The answers are also beneficial just for your thought process. Take a close look at any error messages you're getting. Work your way back to try and spot any mistakes.

Another response to getting stuck is just to start over. If your code is long, it can be discouraging to start from scratch, but that means you don't have to go through the whole thing, picking it apart and wearing out your eyes. Starting over may be more comfortable.

Take a break

Whether you choose to begin again or go through the code with a fine-toothed comb, you should take breaks. When you work on a problem for too long, your brain gets stuck in a groove, and it's difficult to come up with new solutions. Do something that doesn't use the same muscles as coding. Exercise your body instead, take a long shower, lie down for a nap, or bake some cookies. Einstein would often come up with solutions to his problems while he played the violin, and who doesn't want to think a little bit like Einstein?

And here are some tricks given by expert programmers:

List Comprehension Generator Expressions

List comprehension is excellent to use, but there is a downside to using it. Not everything is foolproof, and the most significant disadvantage of using list comprehension is that your whole list is going to have to be placed in the memory at the same time. This is not going to be a problem when your list is small and only contains a few objects. However, when your list is rather extensive, you are only going to be wasting your time.

Using generated expressions is something that came out with Python 2.4 and has changed the number of people who use list comprehension around. When you are using generator expressions, they are not going to load your entire list into the memory bank at once; instead, it is going to create an object that makes it to where only one element that is on the list is loaded at a time.

Should you need to use your entire list for whatever reason, using a generated expression is not the way to go. However, if you are just trying to pass your appearance off for something such as a "for" loop, then the generator function is going to work correctly.

The syntax for a generator expression is going to be the same syntax that you use when using list comprehensions; the only difference is going to be that your parentheses are going to be on the outside of the brackets.

Example

Num = (2, 4, 6, 8)

Squares_under_30 = (num * num for num in num if num * num < 30)

any square that is under 30 will now generate an object which is going to cause each value that is successive to be called on.

For square in squares_ under_ 30:

Print square,

result: '2, 16'

While the code is not shorter like we would like it to be, it is going to be more efficient than using the list comprehension function because it is going to load your list into the memory bank one element at a time. Therefore, making it to where you do not have to agonize about loading it all in at once.

If you want to use this function for a list that contains more elements in it, you do have the option of using the list comprehension technique, but you should only use this if you want to use your entire list at once.

However, you can use whichever method seems right for you in what you are trying to accomplish. It is recommended that you try and use the generator expressions unless you have some reason not to. Still, in the end, you are not going to see any real difference in the list comprehension and generator expressions unless the list that you are working with is extensive.

Keep in mind, however, that a generator expression is only going to require a single set of parentheses. Therefore, if you are calling on a function with a generator expression, you are only going to be necessary to insert a single set of parentheses.

Checking Conditions for Elements in a List

There are going to be conditions that have to be met by the items that are on your list. And there will be times that you are going to want to ensure that these elements are meeting those conditions.

Should you be using Python 2.5, then your code will look similar to this:

Example:

Num = [5, 10, 15, 20, 25, 30]

If [num for num in num if num < 5]:

Print 'two elements that are over five.'

result: there are at least two items that are over five

Should there not be any elements in your list that satisfy your condition, then by default, Python is going to create an empty list and evaluate it as false. But, non-empty lists will be set up and evaluated as true if the condition is met. You do not have to assess every item that is on your list. Instead, you can quit as soon as you find one element that causes your condition to be true.

Python 2.5 has a built-in function known as any, and this function is going to do the same thing that you saw above, only your code is going to be shorter and easier to understand. With any function, it is programmed to bail and give you a true answer after it locates the first element that satisfies your condition. This function can also be used with a generator expression so that you do not have to evaluate every element on your list, and you get your true or false answer back.

Example

Num = [5, 10, 15, 20, 25, 30]

If any (num < 5 for num in num):

Output: success!

If you want to, you do have the option of checking for every element that meets your condition, and if you are not using Python 2.5, then your code is going to look something like this.

Example

Num [5, 10, 15, 20, 25, 30]

If len (num) == len([num for num in num if num < 5]):

Output: success!

It is in this example that the list comprehension technique is used to filter if there are still elements that meet the condition as there were before. It is also checking to see if all of the elements are meeting the requirement. Sadly, this is not an efficient way to complete this technique because there is genuinely no need to check every element that is on your list to see if it satisfies the condition that you have put into place. But, if you are not using Python 2.5, this could end up being the only option that you have of checking the elements for your condition.

As you move back to Python 2.5, there is another function that you can use known as they all function. Just like any function, this function was made to bail once it finds a single element that does not meet the condition, therefore making it to where you are given a false evaluation.

Example

Num = [5, 10, 15, 20, 25, 30]

If all (num < 5 for num in num):

Output: success!

Converting Between a Dict and a List in Python

It is important to remember that your dict is going to be unordered, which will make it seem like the values are not in any meaningful

 order.

Example:

Dictionary = {'b' : 4 'c' : 6 'd': 8}

Dict_into_list = dict.items()

your dict_into_list will now look like this [('b': 4) ('c': 6'), ('d': 8)]

You are going to be taking your two-element list or tuple and changing it into a dict.

Example:

Dict = [('b', 4] ['c', 6], ['d', 8]

Dict _into_ list = dict.items()

your dictionary is now going to look like this: { 'b': 4, 'c' : 6, "d" : 8}

While you may be asking yourself why would you ever want to convert a dict into a list or a list into a dict, let's look at the next tip to understand how helpful knowing how to convert them is.

Python Dictionary Comprehensions

As of this moment, Python does not have any comprehensions built-in for dictionaries. So, if you want a dictionary comprehension, you are going to have to write out your code which is going to produce a piece of code that will give you the results of something readable and going to be reasonably similar to a list comprehension.

From there, you are going to take your list and put it through your generator expression or your list comprehension method before you turn it back into a dict.

Example:

Books = {nonfiction: WorldWarII, fiction: 'BalladofPiney, music: LifeofBobMarley}

Books_at_library = dict([title, genre of book] for title, genere in of book books.iteritems())

```
# Books_at_library result: {WorldWarII: true, BalladofPiney : true,
LifeofBobbyMarley: false}
```

You have no done "dictionary comprehension!" It is not required that you start and end with a dict if you do not want to. You can always do a list or a tuple if that is what you want to use instead.

The code may seem like it is less readable and straightforward than list comprehension, but it is still going to be better than working with a loop that may never end.

Chapter 10.   Performed Python Programming Exercises On Functions, Strings, Lists And Mathematical Calculations

Best Practices

Contained in this chapter will be some of the best practices you can adapt to take your coding to a higher standard. We have touched on this first topic already, but we will expand and reiterate here. First up is naming conventions.

Comments

Here are some best practices for your feedback that will help other readers understand you easier:

• Start with a summary of the sketch and what it will accomplish. Provide any links if it helps the understanding of your design. Try to approach your block comments from a user-friendly stance as much as possible to give a clear idea of what you will be doing.

• Write in the active voice. Use a bright, conversational tone for your writing, as if you were speaking to another person standing next to you.

- For instructions to the user, use the second person, to invoke in the user that they should be the ones to carry out your instructions.

- Use short descriptive phrases rather than complex phrases. It is easier to understand one simple idea at a time.

- Be explicit about what you are doing with your actions. For example: "Next, you'll read the value of the sensor on pin thisPin."

- Avoid phrases or words that are 'fluff' or do not contribute to the explanation, e.g. you see. You'd want to, etc. Instead, skip those words and give a statement that's direct to the point, e.g. set the pins.

- Check your assumptions, make sure you have explained all of your ideas and haven't left something that can only be interpreted 'in your head.'

- Describe every variable or constant with a comment of its purpose either before, or in line with the variable or constant.

- Similarly, explain a block of code that you're about to perform before the instructions are executed, so it's clear what's about to happen.

• Every loop should have comments explaining why this loop exists (e.g. what it is doing), and a verbal explanation of its condition if it's still not clear.

Coding Best Practices

• Follow naming conventions

Do not create one letter variable names! Your naming conventions exist so that you can, at a glance, read your code without having to refer to other places to understand what is going on.

• Write code that is reusable or modular

User-defined functions are a great way to accomplish this. By doing this, you can write a segment of code in just one place and refer to it each time it is necessary. This makes better sense and is much cleaner and simpler to read.

• Write a flow-chart of your sketch before you start coding

Seriously, this cannot be overstated how valuable this step is to write clean code. By knowing all the pieces you will need to accomplish your sketch's task ahead of time conceptually, you can successfully plan and use things like functions in a smart way.

• Keep things organize and together

If you make a function to smooth an analogue sensor, make sure that's all it does. Don't start doing other parts of your code within that function. If your function needs to, you can have it call yet another function to help it accomplish its task. Again think modular (small pieces make a big part).

- Make yourself a toolbox

Make functions that do specific things. Then use your tools as needed in your code.

- Keep your sketches

Even if you think you won't need a sketch you made anymore, keep them. If you need a piece of code that you've already written for another project and you have followed these practices, you can simply snag that piece of code and drop it into the new project you're working. Brilliant!

- Write your functions in a generalized way whenever possible for these exact reasons

It means that if you were making a function to draw a square, make a function to draw a rectangle instead since a square is a special case of a rectangle, where the edges are equal.

- Make sure your functions do what they say they will do

E.g., if it is a function named 'flickerLeds' (pinValue), it better be flickering some LEDs!

- Avoid pointers

We didn't even touch on them in this document, and we are only going to tell you they exist to tell you not to use them unless you're an advanced user. They are the most likely 'tool' to cause the crazy, wrong kinds of problems from happening in your coding, and are notoriously tough for a beginner to use correctly. So avoid them until you are sure you know what you are doing.

- Embrace self-improvement

Understand from day one that as a fledgeling coder that you will grow and improve over time. Use each challenge you come across to try writing new sketches as an opportunity to develop and hone your skills.

- Reach out to the community for help and advice!

There are some fantastic people in our big community of hobbyists that are willing to help you learn and grow as an enthusiast. This is a great way to meet friends and learn so many new ways to do things you may not have thought about previously.

- Try to make things foolproof when you code

Try to make sure your for loops terminate, try to account for unexpected inputs when checking values, try to constrain your data within expected values. These 'tedious' steps are what keeps your program running smooth and bug-free!

- Know how to use debugging tools and techniques

It's a more advanced topic, but learning about debugging tools and techniques for large-scale projects such as robotics, or as a controller for something like a pump mechanism will help expand your knowledge further.

- Write both brackets or both braces at the start then fill in the date in-between

When writing functions, loops or anything with brackets and braces, this trick helps to ensure that you will be closing all of your brackets and braces, preventing unexpected results.

- Try new ways to use your Arduino!

This is how you can develop new skills. When you have more skills, you can think of even more things you can do with the chip! The possibilities with this micro-controller are nearly limitless and are bound only by the limits of your imagination.

More Naming Best Practices

- Functions follow the same rules as variables

The name should start with a lower-case letter, all one word, and additional words are distinguished with capital letters.

- Functions should use verb names to describe their function

E.g. stepMotor(), getValue(), smoothReadings(), etc. All these names explain with an action word what this function should be doing.

• Make the name describe the purpose of the function.

• Make sure the for loop variables are clear on what they represent

Having a variable of x can work, but it offers nothing to the person reading your code for them to understand what that variable is.

Quiz and Workbook

here are significant pointers that can help your learning activity become fruitful.

1. Be positive. Anything new can be daunting – especially a 'foreign' language. Think about learning Korean, Chinese or Spanish, and you won't even want to start. But optimism can make you change your mind. As Master Yoda from "Star Wars' said: "Do, there is no try." Believe that you can do it, and you can. Think about all the benefits you can derive from what you will learn.

2. Python is an extensive program; continue learning. What we have discussed here is only the tip of the iceberg. There are still thousands of complex information about Python that you can learn.

3. If you want to obtain several values from a list, use the 'slice' function, instead of using the index. This is because the 'index' can provide you with a single value only.

4. Assign only integer values to indices. Other number forms are not recognized by Python. Keep in mind that index values start from zero (0).

5. Remember to use the 'help' function whenever necessary. Explore the 'help' function, when in doubt on what to do. A little help from Python can go a long way.

6. Python programming is a dynamic language. Thus, you can experiment and come up with a code of your own to contribute towards its advancement.

7. There are some differences between the Python versions. But don't fret, the program itself has built-in modules and functions that can assist you in solving the problems you can encounter.

8. The interactive shell can promptly return results. That's why it's preferable to open a 'New File' first, before creating your statement. But if you're sure of your code, then, go ahead, and use the interactive shell directly.

9. Separate your multiple statements, in a single line, with semicolons. This is easier and more sensible.

10.   The three 'greater than' signs (>>>) or arrows is a prompt from the interactive shell. You can explore their functionality as you create your statements.

11.   The Python interpreter can act as a calculator. Using your interactive shell, you can compute math problems quickly – and continuously. No sweat!

12.   The # symbol indicates that the statement is a comment. The # sign is placed before the comment, and after the Python statement, so Python won't mistake it as part of the statement or code.

13.   Use the reverse or backslash (\ ) to escape a single quote or double-quotes. Examples of these are contracted words, such as 'don't, "won't", 'aren't'. When using them in Python, they will appear this way: 'don\'t', "won\'t", 'aren\'t'.

14.   A short cut in joining two literal strings (strings literal) is to put them beside each other and enclose each in quotes. Example: 'Clinical' 'Chemistry'. This will give: ClinicalChemistry.

```
>>>
>>> 'Clinical' 'Chemistry'
'ClinicalChemistry'
>>>
>>>
>>> |
```

15.   For modifying immutable data, create a new file. These immutable data include strings, numbers, frozen set, bytes and Tuples. By creating a new file, you can modify, add and remove items from your immutable data.

QUIZ

1. Why do you think multi-line statements are necessary we can simply write a single line, and the program statement will run just fine?

2. List the variable scope types?

3. Start IDLE.

Navigate to the File menu and click New Window.

Type the following:

```
food=['omelet', 'fish','rice']
for j in range(len(food)):
    print("I prefer", food[j])
```

ANSWERS

1. Multi-line statements can help improve formatting/readability of the entire program. Remember, when writing a program always

assume that it is other people who will use and maintain it without your input.

2. The following are the scope types:

i.   Scope containing local names, current function.

ii. Scope containing global names, the scope of the module.

iii. Scope containing built-in names of the outermost scope.

3. The output of this program will be:

I prefer omelette

I prefer fish

I prefer jazz

Chapter 11.   Classes and Objects

Now that we know a little bit more about the basics that come with the Python code, it is time to move on to our first topic of working with classes and objects. These two topics are important because they will make sure that everything in your code stays in the right place. Your objectives are the components which will help define certain parts of the code so that they are organized and easier to understand. The objects all share something in common, and they will be placed into the same class, helping your code to work the way that it should.

There are a lot of things to understand when it comes to working with objects, but the most important part is that whenever you place some objects into the same class, they should have something in common. It adds in a little more order to the whole thing. Think about this process as you organizing the closet. You do this process task it ensures that everything looks beautiful and is easier to find later on.

This is the same idea when you are working on classes. You want to place similar objects into the same class so that it is easier to find them later on. The program will work more efficiently when these objects are similar, rather than randomly placing unrelated objects into the same class.

To make things easier to understand, you should see objects as different aspects and parts of the code that you are writing and then the classes will be like the containers which you will use to store away these objects. You can easily create a class out of anything that you want and then add in similar objects that match up together into that class. You can pick out whatever label that you want to go with the class, just be certain that it makes sense for the type of object that you want to place inside the class. When someone looks at the class, they should have a good idea of what you placed inside of it and the objects should all match that label as well.

If this is a new idea to you and you are just getting started with learning a new coding language, objects and classes are an excellent place to start. It is Because they will help you to learn more while also making sure that everything will stay organized in the code that you are working. As a programmer, it is your job to learn how to create these classes and then get the objects to go inside of them so that the code works the proper way. Let's take a look at how that is going to work in Python.

How to create a new class

Now that we had a little introduction to these objects and classes, it is time for you to learn the steps on how to create your class. You have to do this because you will find that it is hard to get started with anything in Python if you don't do this first. Once you are ready to create the statements that are needed for these classes, you should create a new definition.

You need to place the right keyword first to get this going and then add the name of the class (the name that you are giving to it) right afterwards. This will then be followed with a 'superclass' that you will place inside of the parenthesis. Another thing that you should consider is that at the end of your first line in Python, you need to add a semicolon. Your code will work without it, but this is considered a part of coding etiquette, so you have to make sure that it is present.

Easiest way to understand how it works is to take a look at an example of creating a new class. A good example which will show you how to do this with the Python language is shown below:

```
class Vehicle(object):

#constructor

def_init_(self, steering, wheels, clutch, breaks, gears):

self._steering = steering

self._wheels = wheels

self._clutch = clutch

self._breaks =breaks

self._gears  = gears

#destructor

def_del_(self):
```

```
        print("This is destructor....")

#member functions or methods

def Display_Vehicle(self):

    print('Steering:' , self._steering)

    print('Wheels:', self._wheels)

    print('Clutch:', self._clutch)

    print('Breaks:', self._breaks)

    print('Gears:', self._gears)

#instantiate a vehicle option

myGenericVehicle = Vehicle('Power Steering', 4, 'Super Clutch', 'Disk
Breaks', 5)

myGenericVehicle.Display_Vehicle()
```

Before we move on, take the time to open up your text editor and
write this code down so you won't forget it. As you work on writing
this out, you should notice that there are a few of the basics that we
talked about and explained earlier that will show up in this code. You
will also see the definition of the object and the method, the
destructor function, the different attributes that you will need, and
also some regular functions. Since this is the first code that we will

have a look at, let's break it down a bit so that you can understand and know how to write out codes in this language better.

Class definition

The first thing we will talk about is the class definition. You need to write out the object instantiation and then the class definition so that your syntax is proper when put inside the code. These are important because they are the part of the code that will tell your compiler what it should do and which commands are essential. If you want to invoke the new class definition inside of the code, you just have to use the 'object.attribute' or the 'object.method()' function and it will work flawlessly.

Special attributes

The next thing that you can focus on in the above code is the special attributes that you want the code to recognize for you. You may want to take a closer look at these because they will add a lot to your code and will help make it work better. These special attributes will give you some peace of mind because you can know when the attribute will be seen, and you can make sure that it is used in the right way to prevent the code from getting messed up. There are a lot of good attributes that can be used in Python, but some of the ones that you really should pay attention to as a beginner include:

- __bases__

This is considered a tuple that contains any of the superclasses

- __module__

You are going to find the name of the module, and it will also hold your classes.

- __name__

This will hold on to the class name.

- __doc__

This is where you are going to find the reference string inside the document for your class.

- __dict__

This is going to be the variable for the dict. Inside the class name.

How to access members of a class

Now we need to look at how you can access members of a class. To make sure that your text editor and compiler can recognize a class and execute the parts that you want, you must make sure that this code is correctly set up to access all the members of that class. You will be happy to know that there are a few options you can use to make this happen, and all of them will work out well, but the 'accessor' method is the most popular and the most efficient one to work

To help you understand how this works, let's take a look at the following code to make it easier.

```python
class Cat(object)

itsAge = None

itsWeight = None

itsName = None

#set accessor function use to assign values to the fields or member vars

def setItsAge(self, itsAge):

self.itsAge = itsAge

def setItsWeight(self, itsWeight):

self.itsWeight = itsWeight

def setItsName(self, itsName):

self.itsName =itsName

#get accessor function use to return the values from a field

def getItsAge(self):

return self.itsAge

def getItsWeight(self):
```

```python
return self.itsWeight

def getItsName(self):

return self.itsName

objFrisky = Cat()

objFrisky.setItsAge(5)

objFrisky.setItsWeight(10)

objFrisky.setItsName("Frisky")

print("Cats Name is:", objFrisky.getItsname())

print("Its age is:", objFrisky.getItsAge())

print("Its weight is:", objFrisky.getItsName())
```

Make sure to open up and place this in your compiler before we move on. If you ask the compiler to run this, you should get some results that show up right away. The results that you get will include that the name of the cat is Frisky (or whatever name you would like to add in there) and that the age is five while the weight is 10. This is the information that we placed into the code, but you can add different names and different numbers in there if that works out better for you. Try out a few different options to see what will work and learn how you can make it work for you.

As you can see, classes and objects are easy to work. These are some of the best ways you can use to take care of the information that is inside of your code. You can create the class and then add the objects that you want and then match them into the class that you created. This will keep your coding nice and organized just like the way that you want it, and it also makes sure the program will work.

Chapter 12.   The Best Machine Learning and Data Analysis Libraries with Python

Python is going to be one of the best options that we are able to go with when it is time to handle data analysis with machine learning. But the standard library that we will see with Python is often not going to have all of the features and the functions that we need in order to handle this process. Learning how to work with the different libraries that come with Python will be one of the best things that you can do overall, so let's dive in and see which libraries work the best with Python and machine learning, and which ones are going to help you to handle your data analysis models.

The NumPy and SciPy Library

The first two libraries that we are going to explore here are going to be the NumPy, or Numeric and Scientific Computation, and the SciPy library. NumPy is a useful library to learn about because it is going to help us lay down some of the basic premises that are needed for any kind of scientific computing that we wish to do with Python. It is also going to be there to help us grab the functions that we need, many of which are precompiled and fast enough to help out with any and all mathematical and numerical routines.

In addition to some of the listed benefits that we have above, NumPy is also able to help us optimize some of the programming that we want to do with Python. The way that it can do this is to add in a few powerful data structures along the way. what this does is makes it easier for us to efficiently compute the arrays and the matrices that we have, especially when one or both of these are considered multi-dimensional.

Then we have SciPy, or Scientific Python, which is going to come with NumPy in many cases. Often you can't get one to work well without the other because they share many features. When you are working with SciPy, you are able to gain that competitive edge even more than just using NumPy on its own. This happens when you try to enhance some of the useful functions for regression, minimization, and so much more.

The Pandas Library

The next library that we need to spend some time on when we are looking for help with one of our data analytics projects is going to be known as Pandas, or the Python Data Analysis Library. You will find that the name gives away why this library is so important, and why we need to spend some time working with this as well.

Pandas are going to be one of the tools that work with Python, and it is also open-sourced so you can download it and start working with it without any problems. It is going to provide us with some great and easy data structures to work with, and it has a lot of high-performance abilities that will help as well. In fact, you will find that the Pandas library is able to help us out with all of the different programming things that we want to do when it comes to finishing the data analysis.

You are able to work with this library in particular when you want to add in some new structures of data and some new tools to help with the data analysis. And you will find that this work regardless of the kind of project that you would like to complete. There are many industries and companies that are fond of working with this kind of library to help them with things like finance, social science, engineering, and statistics to name a few.

The best part about using this library is that it is adaptable, which helps us to get more work done. It also works with any kind of data that you were able to collect for it, including uncategorized, messy, unstructured, and incomplete data. Even once you have the data, this library is going to step in and help provide us with all of the tools that we need to slice, reshape, merge, and more all of the sets of data we have.

Pandas are going to come with a variety of features that makes it perfect for data science. Some of the best features that come with the Pandas library from Python will include:

1. You can use the Pandas library to help reshape the structures of your data.
2. You can use the Pandas library to label series, as well as tabular data, to help us see an automatic alignment of the data.
3. You can use the Pandas library to help with heterogeneous indexing of the data, and it is also useful when it comes to systematic labeling of the data as well.
4. You can use this library because it can hold onto the capabilities of identifying and then fixing any of the data that is missing.
5. This library provides us with the ability to load and then save data from more than one format.

6. You can easily take some of the data structures that come out of Python and NumPy and convert them into the objects that you need to Pandas objects.

The Matplotlib Library

When you are working with some of the visuals that are needed in data analysis, you will find that the matplotlib library is one of the best ones that you would like to work with. This helps you to really visualize and understand all of the information that you have collected and really helps you to figure out the relationships that are going to come up with your models. It is also going to make it more efficient to see how the insights are going to be worth your time.

Working with these visuals is going to be so important. Depending on the kind of data that is in your models and that you have been working with the whole time, you will find that these visuals are going to make it easier to see what information you have gathered, and how the different parts are going to work when you try to combine them together.

This is one of the areas where you will see that this library is going to be useful. It is basically going to be a 2D plotting library that you are able to use with Python, and it can really help us by producing figures that are publication quality in a lot of formats. You will also see that it can offer you a variety of interactive environments to work with that can handle many platforms based on your needs. This library can be used with scripts from Python, Jupyter, IPython, and more to help get things done.

The way that this library is going to be able to help us with data science is that it is able to generate a lot of the visualizations that we need to handle all of our data, and the results that we get out of the data. This library is able to help with generating scatterplots, error charts, bar charts, power spectra, histograms, and plots to name a few. If you need to have some kind of chart or graph to go along with your data analysis, make sure to check out what the matplotlib option can do for you.

The Scikit-Learn Library

While we are on the topic, we need to spend a few minutes looking at the Scikit-Learn library and how well it is able to handle some of the machine learning and data analysis work that you want to do with Python. This one is going to have a ton of algorithms that work well with machine learning and these algorithms can often fit under the idea of supervised and unsupervised machine learning problems that are low to medium scale. This means that there are a lot of potential uses and applications to make all of this work.

Out of some of the other libraries that we have been able to bring up in this guidebook, and this chapter, so far, the Scikit-Learn library is going to be one of the best to help us handle a lot of different things when it comes to machine learning. This package, in particular, is going to focus on helping us to bring some more machine learning to some of those who may not be professionals in coding and the other parts of this that they need to focus on.

When you are working with the Python language, and working with the Scikit-Learn library to help out with some of the machine learning, you will find that the main emphasis that we are going to see will be on things like how easy it is to use, the performance of the model, a bit on the documentation, and the consistency that we are able to get to show up on the API.

Another benefit that we are going to see when it comes to this library is that it is not going to have a lot of dependencies, which makes it easier to work with, and it is relatively easy to distribute. You will find that this is a library that will show up in many settings, whether they are academic or commercial. This library is going to show us an interface that is concise and consistent and that we can use for many machine learning algorithms and help us handle the machine learning and data science that we would like.

The TensorFlow Library

We can also work with the library that is known as TensorFlow. This is actually considered one of the best libraries out there that works with Python and can handle the work that you want to do with data science. This is a library that was originally released by the Google

Brain Team. It was written out mostly with the help of the C++ language, which is a bit different but it comes with some of the bindings in Python, so you will be able to still use the language that you have been learning without having to worry about it.

One of the best features that you will see with the TensorFlow library is that it is going to have a flexible architecture that is nice for allowing the programmer to deploy it with one or more GPU's or CPUs on your device whether that is a server, a mobile, or a desktop device. And you can do all of this with the same API the whole time.

Not many, if really any, of the other libraries that we are working with inside of this chapter are able to come close to making this kind of claim. This library can also add in some more unique features in that it was developed by the Google Brain project, and it is not going to miss out on a lot of the features that you want.

One thing to keep in mind with this though is that you will need to spend a bit more of your time on this library in order to learn the API of this library compared to what we see with the other libraries. It only takes a few minutes to find out that you are able to really get the hang of it pretty quickly as well. And it is going to work when it is time to implement the design that you want to have with your network, without having to fight through the API as we will find with the other options.

The Keras Library

Keras is going to be an open-sourced library form Python that is able to help you to build up your own neural networks, at a high level of the interface. It is going to be pretty minimalistic, which makes it easier to work with, and the coding on this library is going to be simple and straightforward, while still adding in some of the high-level extensibility that you need. It is going to work either TensorFlow or Theano along with CNTK as the backend to make this work better. We can remember that the API that comes with Keras is designed for humans to use, rather than humans, which makes it easier to use and puts the experience of the user right in front.

Keras is going to work with all of the best-known practices at the time when it is necessary to reduce the cognitive load. This Python library is going to offer us a consistent and simple API that will help us to minimize how many actions that the user has to do for the different parts of the code that are common, and it also helps to provide feedback that is actionable and clear if you do end up with an error on the code.

In this library, we may find that the model will be understood more like a sequence, or we can change it up and make it a standalone or a graph. You can even work with fully-configurable modules that you are able to put together with only a few restrictions at the time.

Options like cost functions, initialization schemes, activation functions, optimizers, and neural layers are all going to be examples of the modules that can stand alone but then can be put together when you would like to create your own model. You will then find that Keras can help you to create some of these new modules, and the existing modules that are already there can provide us with examples to work with as well if we are just starting with it.

The Theano Library

Theano is another great library to work with during data science, and it is often seen as one of the highly-rated libraries to get this work done. In this library, you will get the benefit of defining, optimizing, and then evaluating many different types of mathematical expressions that come with multi-dimensional arrays in an efficient manner. This library is able to use lots of GPUs and perform symbolic differentiation in a more efficient manner.

Theano is a great library to learn how to use, but it does come with a learning curve that is pretty steep, especially for most of the people who have learned how to work with Python because declaring the variables and building up some of the functions that you want to work with will be quite a bit different from the premises that you learn in Python.

However, this doesn't mean that the process is impossible. It just means that you need to take a bit longer to learn how to make this happen. With some good tutorials and examples, it is possible for someone who is brand new to Theano to get this coding all done. Many great libraries that come with Python, including Padas and NumPy, will be able to make this a bit easier as well.

As we can see, there are a ton of great libraries that work well with the Python language that can also be added to the project that we do with machine learning and data analysis. Each of these will have their own benefits to work with, and you can pick and choose which ones have the features, the algorithms and the other parts that you need to have a really strong data project in no time.

Chapter 13. How Machine Learning is Applied in the Real World

It's one thing to talk about machine learning in the abstract. To get a better handle on machine learning, we also want to understand how it's being used in businesses and other large organizations today to perform useful functions. First, let's understand where machine learning fits into the overall framework of computer science and artificial intelligence.

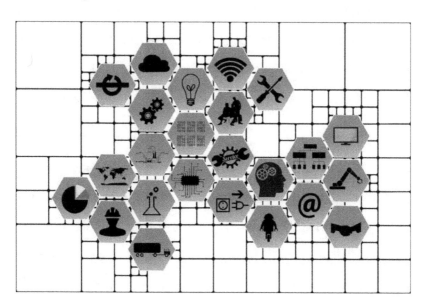

When Does Machine Learning Work?

When faced with a problem that is suitable for the deployment of a computer system, the first thing that you should ask about the question is whether or not it is rigid and unchanging, or is this something that requires an adaptive system?

At first glance, this seems like a simple question. For example, suppose that you were considering a ballistics program for the military. Ballistics follow the laws of physics. These are precisely known, and so it should be a simple matter to do calculations to get the accurate results that are desired. Hardcoded computer programs can be used to predict how things will work in real situations. Indeed, as soon as Newton's laws were known in the 17th and 18th centuries, armies were using people to do the calculations by hand, and this helped to revolutionize warfare and military efficiency. Today it's done even better and faster using powerful computer technology.

But a recent example shows that there is often more to any situation than meets the eye. Consider an EKG, which can give a doctor a picture of the performance of the heart. An EKG is used to diagnose a heart attack, arrhythmias, and many other problems. It's very narrowly focused, and patterns on the EKG are associated with specific conditions. Health professionals are trained to recognize those patterns, and they can study an EKG chart and determine which patients need medical intervention and which don't. This is as straightforward as the ballistics problem.

However, when artificially intelligent systems were developed using machine learning to study EKGs, it was found that they outperformed doctors by a significant margin. The machine learning systems that have been developed can predict which patients will die within a year with 85% accuracy. For comparison, doctors can make the same prediction with 65% to at most 80% accuracy.

The key here is the difference. When there are EKGs that look entirely normal to the human eye—the machine learning system can determine that in fact, they are not healthy. The engineers that designed the system can't explain it. They don't know why or how the machine learning system makes its predictions. But the way it works, generally speaking, is that the machine learning system can detect patterns in the data that human minds cannot detect.

This example serves to illustrate that adaptive learning can be used in nearly every situation. Even in ballistics, there may be many different factors that human engineers have not adequately accounted for. Who knows what they are, it could be the humidity, wind, or other factors. The bet is that although line-by-line coded software works very well in deterministic situations, adaptive software that is not programmed and only trained with data will do better.

Complex and Adaptive

When there is any situation where experience—that is exposed to more data—can improve performance, machine learning is called for.

If the data is involved, this is another situation where machine learning can shine. Think about how the human mind can handle mathematical problems. Even two-dimensional problems in calculus and differential equations are severe for most people, and also the smartest people struggle while learning it for the first time. It gets even more complicated when you move to three dimensions, and the more complexity that is added, the harder it is for people to digest.

If you are looking at a data set, you are going to be facing the same situation. If we have a small data set of 20 items, each with three fields and an output, a human operator might be able to extract a relationship between the inputs and outputs. They could even do linear regression by hand or plug it into a simple program like Microsoft Excel. Also simply eyeballing, the data can reveal the relationships.

But the more data you add to the problem, the less able a human operator can determine what the relationships are. The same problem with output but 20 inputs might make it very difficult. If there are no outputs, and you ask human operators to see if there are any patterns in the data, it might become virtually impossible.

One way that we get around complexity in the real world is to program computers in the standard way. This helps humans get around many significant data problems and solving problems that would involve tedious work. Consider whether prediction, early efforts at predicting the weather or modelling the climate were based on standard line-by-line coding, using the laws of physics and inputs believed to be distinguished by the operator.

However, when there is a large amount of complexity is a problem, such as predicting the weather, this is a signal that machine learning is probably going to outperform any method by a wide margin. Think about climate modelling. The scientists and programmers are going to make estimates of what factors (such as carbon dioxide level) are essential.

But using machine learning, merely training the system on raw data, the system would probably detect patterns in the data that human observers don't even know are there. And it would likely build an even more accurate method that would be better at making future predictions.

To summarize, when you have a problem that is adaptive and complex, then it is well suited for machine learning. But there is a third component, and this is big data.

The Role of Big Data

Over the past two or three decades, there has been a quiet revolution in computing power that went unnoticed at first. Developments in technology made it possible to develop more storage capacity, and the costs of this storage capacity have continually dropped. This phenomenon, combined with the internet to make it easy for organizations that are large and small to collect enormous amounts of information and store it. The concept of big data was born.

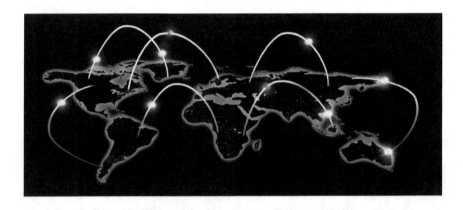

Big data is, of course, large amounts of data. However, experts characterize big data in four ways.

Merely having a static set of large amounts of data is not useful unless you can quickly access it. Big data is characterized by the "four V's".

- Volume: Huge amounts of data are being created and stored by computer systems throughout the world.
- Velocity: The speed of data movement continues to increase. Rate of data means that computer systems can gather and analyze more substantial amounts of data more quickly.

- Variety: Collection methods from different sources also characterize big data. For example, a consumer profile can include data from a person's behaviour while online. Still, it will also include mobile data from their smartphone, and data from wearable technology like smartwatches.

- Veracity: The truthfulness of the data is important. Do business leaders trust the data they are using? If the data is erroneous, it's not going to be useful.

The key to focus on here is that big data plays a central role in machine learning. In fact, without adequate amounts of accurate (truthful) data that can be accessed quickly, machine learning wouldn't work. The fundamentals of machine learning were developed decades ago. Still, it really wasn't until we moved into the 21st century that the ability to collect and move data around caught up to what was known about machine learning. The arrival of big data is what turned machine learning from an academic curiosity into something real that could be deployed in the real world to get real results.

Where Does Machine Learning Fit In?

Now that we understand the relationship of machine learning to big data let's see where machine learning fits in with other concepts in computer science. We begin with artificial intelligence. Artificial intelligence is the overarching concept that entails computer systems that can learn and get better with experience. The following general characteristics can characterize artificial intelligence:

- The ability to learn from data.
- The ability to get better from experience
- The ability to reason.
- It is completely general, as the human brain. So, it can learn anything and can learn multiple tasks.

Machine learning is a subset of artificial intelligence. Rather than being completely general and engaging in human-like reasoning, machine learning is focused on a specific task.

There are four major areas of machine learning, and within each of these, there are specialities:

- Supervised learning–good for predictions of future outputs.
- Unsupervised learning–good for classifying objects
- Reinforcement learning–a type of learning that encourages ideal behaviour by giving rewards.
- Deep learning–A computer system that attempts to mimic the human brain using a neural network
- It can be trained to perform a specific task.

Some Applications of Machine Learning

We have touched on a few ways that machine learning is used in the real world. To get a better feel for machine learning and how it's applied, let's go through some of the most impactful ways that it is being used.

Crimes and Criminal Activity

When you think about machine learning, think patterns. One very practical use of machine learning is exposing a system to past data from criminal activity.

This data can contain many different fields or features. They could include:

- Type of crime committed.

- Location of the crime.

- Time of day.

- Information about the perpetrator or perpetrators

- Information about the victim.

- Weapons used.

- Day of the week and day of the month

- Year when the crime occurred

By studying the data and looking for hidden patterns, a machine learning system can be built to predict the incidents of future crimes. This doesn't mean that it is going to be able to predict a specific crime "there will be a robbery at 615 main street at 6 PM", but rather it will predict overall patterns of criminal activity.

This activity might vary in ways that even experienced law enforcement officers are unable to predict–reflect on the EKG example.

How can this help in the real world? It can help law enforcement agencies deploy resources more efficiently. Even if they don't understand why a given system is making the predictions it's making, they can benefit by moving more law enforcement resources into areas that the system is telling them are going to experience more criminal activity. This can help police and emergency personnel respond to crimes more rapidly, and it can also help deter crime with a greater police presence.

Hospital Staffing

Hospital staffing suffers from a similar problem. Human managers attempt to guess when most doctors and nurses are needed and where they should be deployed. While these estimates are reasonably accurate, improvements can be made by deploying a system that uses machine learning. Again, think back to the EKG example–a doctor is pretty good, giving results with 65-80% accuracy. But the machine learning system is even better with 85%, picking out situations the doctors miss. That kind of difference can be a large matter of life or death when it comes to efficiently allocate staff in a large hospital.

To put together systems of this type, large medical organizations tracked the locations and movements of nurses. This allowed them to provide input data to the system, which was able to identify areas of waste. As a simple example, it might have discovered that a large number of nurses were idle on the 7th floor. At the same time, there were not enough nurses in a different ward of the hospital, and so patients there were not getting needed attention, and some may have died as a result.

The Lost Customer Problem

For a business, a loyal customer is worth their weight in gold–or far more. A loyal customer is one that is going to return to make repeated purchases. Or even better, they will subscribe. What do you think is more valuable to companies like Verizon and T-Mobile, selling you the phone, or the fact that you sign up for possibly years of regular monthly payments?

Since loyal customers keep business profitable, learning why customers leave is very important. Even just a decade ago, this had to be done using guesswork. But now, vast sums of data have been collected on customers by large corporations. Preventing their customers from switching to a different company is something they are heavily focused on. And machine learning is enabling them to look for patterns in the data that can help them identify why a customer leaves, and even predict when a customer is about to leave.

This data can include basic demographics, usage patterns, attempts to contact customer support, and so on. The first step where machine learning can be used is that customers that have switched to another company can be identified. Then the system can learn what underlying patterns there are that would enable it to predict what customers are going to leave in the future.

Another way that this data can be used is to study retention efforts. Once a customer is identified that is likely to leave, perhaps they can be offered a special deal. For example, a cell phone company could offer a large discount on a new phone if they sign up for another two-year contract. Or they could offer them free minutes or unlimited data.

Over time, more data is going to be collected. Machine learning can be applied again, this time to determine which methods work the best and what patterns exist–in other words, what method works best for what customers. Maybe you will find that customers of different ages, genders, or living in different locations, or working at different types of jobs, will respond in different ways to inducements offered to retain the customer.

This type of analysis will allow the company to tailor it's responses to each additional customer, improving the odds that they can keep the customer. The customers themselves will be happier, feeling that the company is responsible for their personal needs. The data will also help the company anticipate future market changes and help them adapt using predictive analytics.

Robotics

Using machine learning to develop better and more capable robotics is a huge area of inquiry. Robotics started simple, performing rote tasks that don't require a huge amount of thought. For example, in the 1980s robotics were introduced on assembly lines to put in a screw or do some other task. The problem then was simple, and the robot would perform a small number of exact, rote tasks that could be pre-programmed.

Now robotics are becoming more sophisticated, using cognitive systems to perform many tasks that are tedious but were once thought to be something that only human beings could do. For example, recently, robots have been developed that can work as fast-food cooks. This is going to have major implications for unskilled labour because there are two factors at play in the current environment. Activism is pushing up wages for hourly employees doing unskilled labour, while the costs of robotics that can perform the same tasks are dropping. Moreover, the abilities of the robots to perform these tasks continually improves.

A breakeven point is going to be reached. That is the cost of buying and operating a robot will be less than the costs of hiring a human employee. The robot will never waver inefficiency, it won't require the payment of employment taxes, and it's never going to file a lawsuit or allege discrimination. From the employer's perspective, automation is going to be preferable, and this trend probably can't be stopped.

Over the past year, many sophisticated robots have been revealed to the public. Boston Dynamics, for example, has built robots that can work in warehouses. They can identify packages that need to be moved, pick them up, and then place them where they need to be. At present, the only thing preventing widespread adaptation of this type of technology is cost.

This means that a sophisticated computer system has to be in place in the robot that includes many machine learning systems. The machine learning systems will include movements required to perform the task and the ability to avoid running into someone or another robot. Another form of artificial intelligence, computer vision, plays a significant role in the development of robotics, helping it to identify objects (and people) that are in the robot's environment.

Since modern robotics is using machine learning, the ability of the robots to do their jobs and navigate the environments they are in will improve with time.

Chapter 14.   Multithreading

Threads are lightweight processes that perform specific actions in a program, and they are part of a process themselves. These threads can work in parallel with each other in the same way as two individual applications can.

Since threads in the same process share the memory space for the variables and the data, they can exchange information and communicate efficiently. Also, threads need fewer resources than methods. That's why they're often called lightweight processes.

How A Thread Works

A thread has a beginning or a start, a working sequence and an end. But it can also be stopped or put on hold at any time. The latter is also called sleep.

There are two types of threads: Kernel Threads and User Threads. Kernel threads are part of the operating system, whereas the programmer manages user threads. That's why we will focus on user threads in this book.

In Python, a thread is a class that we can create instances of. Each of these instances then represents an individual thread which we can start, pause or stop. They are all independent of each other, and they can perform different operations at the same time.

For example, in a video game, one thread could be rendering all the graphics, while another thread processes the keyboard and mouse inputs. It would be unthinkable to perform these tasks one after the other serially.

Starting Threads

To work with threads in Python, we will need to import the respective library threading.

```
import threading
```

Then, we need to define our target function. This will be the function that contains the code that our thread shall be executing. Let's just keep it simple for the beginning and write a hello world function.

```
import threading


def hello():

    print("Hello World!")
```

```
t1 = threading.Thread(target=hello)
```

```
t1.start()
```

After we have defined the function, we create our first thread. For this, we use the class Thread of the imported threading module. As a parameter, we specify the target to be the hello function. Notice that we don't put parentheses after our function name here since we are not calling it but just referring to it. By using the start method, we put our thread to work, and it executes our function.

Start VS Run

In this example, we used the function start to put our thread to work. Another alternative would be the function run. The difference between these two functions gets important when we are dealing with more than just one thread.

When we use the run function to execute our threads, they run serially one after the other. They wait for each other to finish. The start function puts all of them to work simultaneously.

The following example demonstrates this difference quite well.

```
import threading
```

```python
def function1():

    for x in range(1000):

        print("ONE")


def function2():

    for x in range(1000):

        print("TWO")



t1 = threading.Thread(target=function1)

t2 = threading.Thread(target=function2)

t1.start()

t2.start()
```

When you run this script, you will notice that the output alternates between ONEs and TWOs. Now if you use the run function instead of the start function, you will see 1000 times ONE followed by 1000 times TWO. This shows you that the threads are run serially and not in parallel.

One more thing that you should know is that the application itself is also the main thread, which continues to run in the background. So while your threads are running, the code of the script will be executed unless you wait for the threads to finish.

Waiting For Threads

If we want to wait for our threads to finish before we move on with the code, we can use the join function.

```
import threading


def function():

    for x in range(500000):

        print("HELLO WORLD!")
```

```
t1 = threading.Thread(target=function)

t1.start()


 print("THIS IS THE END!")
```

If you execute this code, you will start printing the text "HELLO WORLD!" 500,000 times. But what you will notice is that the last print statement gets executed immediately after our thread starts and not after it ends.

```
t1 = threading.Thread(target=function)

t1.start()




t1.join()


 print("THIS IS THE END!")
```

By using the join function here, we wait for the thread to finish before we move on with the last print statement. If we want to set a maximum time that we want to expect, we just pass the number of seconds as a parameter.

```python
t1 = threading.Thread(target=function)

t1.start()

t1.join(5)

print("THIS IS THE END!")
```

In this case, we will wait for the thread to finish but only a maximum of five seconds. After this time has passed, we will proceed with the code.

Notice that we are only waiting for this particular thread. If we had other threads running at the same time, we would have to call the join function on each of them to wait for all of them.

Thread Classes

Another way to build our threads is to create a class that inherits the Thread class. We can then modify the run function and implement our functionality. The start function is also using the code from the run function, so we don't have to worry about that.

```python
import threading


class MyThread(threading.Thread):



    def __init__(self, message):

        threading.Thread.__init__(self)

        self.message = message




    def run(self):

        for x in range(100):
```

```
    print(self.message)
```

```
mt1 = MyThread("This is my thread message!")
```

```
mt1.start()
```

It is the same, but it offers more modularity and structure if you want to use attributes and additional functions.

Synchronizing Threads

Sometimes you are going to have multiple threads running that all try to access the same resource. This may lead to inconsistencies and problems. To prevent such things, there is a concept called locking. One thread is closing all of the other threads, and they can only continue to work when the lock is removed.

I came up with the following quite a trivial example. It seems a bit abstract, but you can still get the concept here.

```
import threading
 import time
```

```python
x = 8192


def halve():

    global x

    while(x > 1):

        x /= 2

        print(x)

        time.sleep(1)

    print("END!")


def double():

    global x
```

```python
    while(x < 16384):

        x *= 2

        print(x)

        time.sleep(1)

    print("END!")


t1 = threading.Thread(target=halve)

t2 = threading.Thread(target=double)



t1.start()

t2.start()
```

Here we have two functions and the variable x that starts at the value 8192. The first function halves the number as long as it is greater than one, whereas the second function doubles the number as long as it is less than 16384.

Also, I've imported the module time to use the function of sleep. This function puts the thread to sleep for a couple of seconds (in this case one second). So it pauses. We just do that, so that we can better track what's happening.

When we now start two threads with these target functions, we will see that the script won't come to an end. The halve function will continually decrease the number, and the double feature will constantly increase it.

With locking, we can now let one function finish before the next function starts. Of course, in this example, this is not very useful, but we can do the same thing in much more complex situations.

```
import threading
import time
```

```
x = 8192
```

```
lock = threading.Lock()
```

```python
def halve():

    global x, lock

    lock.acquire()

    while(x > 1):

        x /= 2

        print(x)

        time.sleep(1)

    print("END!")

    lock.release()


def double():

    global x, lock
```

```python
    lock.acquire()

    while(x < 16384):

        x *= 2

        print(x)

        time.sleep(1)

    print("END!")

    lock.release()



t1 = threading.Thread(target=halve)

t2 = threading.Thread(target=double)



t1.start()
```

t2.start()

So here we added a couple of elements. First of all, we defined a Lock object. It is part of the threading module, and we need this object to manage the locking.

Now, when we want to try to lock the resource, we use the function acquire. If the lock was already closed by someone else, we wait until it is rereleased before we continue with the code. However, if the lock is free, we lock it ourselves and release it at the end using the release function.

Here, we start both functions with a locking attempt. The first function that gets executed will lock the other function and finish its loop. After that, it will release the lock, and the other function can do the same.

So the number will be halved until it reaches the number one and then it will be doubled until it reaches the number 16384.

Semaphores

Sometimes we don't want to lock a resource completely but just limit it to a certain amount of threads or accesses. In this case, we can use so-called semaphores.

To demonstrate this concept, we will look at another very abstract example.

```python
import threading
import time


semaphore = threading.BoundedSemaphore(value=5)


def access(thread_number):

    print("{}: Trying access..."

        .format(thread_number))

    semaphore.acquire()

    print("{}: Access granted!"

        .format(thread_number))
```

```python
    print("{}: Waiting 5 seconds..."

        .format(thread_number))

    time.sleep(5)

    semaphore.release()

    print("{}: Releasing!"

        .format(thread_number))


for thread_number in range(10):

    t = threading.Thread(target=access,

            args=(thread_number,))

    t.start()
```

We first use the BoundedSemaphore class to create our semaphore object. The parameter value determines how many parallel accesses we allow. In this case, we choose five.

With our access function, we try to access the semaphore. Here, this is also done with the acquire function. If less than five threads are utilizing the semaphore, we can acquire it and continue with the code. But when it's full, we need to wait until some other thread frees up one space.

When we run this code, you will see that the first five threads will immediately run the code, whereas the remaining five threads will need to wait five seconds until the first threads release the semaphore.

This process makes a lot of sense when we have limited resources or limited computational power in a system, and we want to limit access to it.

Events

With events, we can manage our threads even better. We can pause a thread and wait for a certain event to happen, to continue it.

Import threading

event = threading.Event()

```python
def function():

    print("Waiting for event...")

    event.wait()

    print("Continuing!")


thread = threading.Thread(target=function)

thread.start()


x = input("Trigger event?")
if(x == "yes"):

    event.set()
```

To define an event, we use the Event class of the threading module. Now we define our function which waits for our event. This is done with the wait function. So we start the thread, and it waits.

Then we ask the user if he wants to trigger the event. If the answer is yes, we trigger it by using the set function. Once the event is triggered, our function no longer waits and continues with the code.

Chapter 15.   Windows

Windows refers to a group of many different graphical operating system families that are produced, marketed, and distributed by the Microsoft group. Every family in this group cares for a given part of the computing world. Some of the active Microsoft Windows families include the following: Windows IoT and Windows NT — which contains other subfamilies such as Windows CE (Windows Embedded Compact) or Windows Server. Microsoft Windows families now defunct include the following: Windows Phone, Windows Mobile, and Windows 9x.

The operating environment now known as Windows was introduced in 1985, on the 20th of November by Microsoft. The release was to serve as a graphical operating system shell for the then MS-DOS as a response to the growing rate of interest in GUIs (Graphical user interfaces). Over time, Microsoft Windows dominated the PC (personal computer) market across the world, grossing over 90% of the market share worldwide, and overthrowing Apple's Mac OS, which was released earlier in 1984.

Windows and Python

In this section, we would consider the relationship between Windows and Python.

- Installing Python on Windows:

Contrary to many of the services and systems operating Unix, Windows doesn't traditionally need Python, and as such, contains no pre-installed version of the programming language. Albeit, Windows installers known as MSI packages have been compiled the CPython team following every release of Python across the years. With the ongoing evolution of Python, some of the platforms that used to support it previously no longer support it as a result of the absence of a user base or developers. PEP 11 contains details about the platforms that no longer support Python.

Windows 3.x and DOS are since deprecated, dating as early as Python 2.0. For this reason, codes peculiar to these platforms were omitted following the release of Python 2.1.

Up until version 2.5, Python was still supported on platforms like Windows ME, 98, and 95, even though a deprecation warning was usually raised during the installation. However, from Python 2.6 and every other release until the time if this writing, the compatibly to those platforms ended, and future releases are expected to share compatibility solely to the Windows NT family.

It still supports Windows CE

The Python interpreter is installed by the Cygwin installer as well (cf. Cygwin package source, Maintainer releases).

- Optional bundles:

Asides the standard CPython distribution, specific modified packages include extra functionality. Shown below are some of the widely known versions as well as their essential characteristics:

· ActivePython:

This is an installer that is compatible across multiple platforms and contains PyWin32 and documentation.

· Enthought Python Distribution:

Widely known modules like PyWin32, as well as the documentation peculiar to them, and a tool suite for developing extensible applications in Python.

Keep in mind that the packages mentioned above have a much higher tendency of installing an older version of Python.

- **Python Configuration:**

To be able to execute Python codes flawlessly, you would find that specific changes needed to be made to the environment in Windows.

Excursus: Setting up environment variables:

There is a built-in dialogue in Windows used in changing the environment variables according to a guide, which mainly applies to the classical view in XP. To start, right-click on the My Computer icon on your Windows system, and click on properties. Next, click to open the Advanced tab, and select the button marked Environment Variables.

Put simply, the path used is:

My computer → Properties → Advanced → Environment Variables

The system and user variables can be added or modified in this dialogue. To alter the system, non-restricted access to the machine is required. That is administrator rights.

An alternative way to add variables into the environment is to make use of the set command:

set PYTHONPATH=%PYTHONPATH%;C:\My_python_lib

To ensure this setting stays permanent, you can try adding the corresponding command line onto your autoexec.bat. In this file, msconfig assumes the role of a graphical interface.

Checking out environmental variables can be a relatively straightforward process if done correctly. The strings automatically wrapped into the per cent signs would be expanded by the command prompt, as shown below:

echo %PATH%

- Locating the Python executable:

Asides making use of the start menu automatically developed for the Python interpreter, it is possible to execute Python from the DOS prompt. To ensure this technique works, you would have to set up the %path% environment variable to add to the directory of the Python distribution, limited using a semicolon form another entry. A sample variable would typically follow after this fashion, given that the first two entries are default in Windows:

C:\WINDOWS\system32;C:\WINDOWS;C:\Python25

Entering Python into your command prompt would start up the Python interpreter. As such, you would be able to run Python scripts using options in the command line.

- Locating Modules:

The libraries in Python, including site-packages folders, are usually stored in the installation directory in Python. As such, if you have your program installed into c:\python\, the default library can be found in the path: C:\Python\Lib\, while the third-party modules would typically be saved in the path: C:\Python\Lib\site-packages\.

Sys.path is populated in Windows through the following:

At the start, an empty entry is introduced that is similar to that of the present directory.

Should the environment variable PYTHONPATH be available as was described in environment variables, the next thing to be added are its entries. Keep in mind that paths in the variable have to be spaced using semicolons in Windows; this would serve to tell them apart from the colon, which the drivers use, as in C:\.

Other added application paths can be introduced into the registry in the form of subkeys of the path \SOFTWARE\Python\PythonCore{version}\PythonPath, placed under the hives HKEY_LOCAL_MACHINE and HKEY_CURRENT_USER. The subkeys which are comprised of path strings delimited by semicolons as their default values would make every path to be included in the sys.path. Take note that every installer is known to make use of HKLM alone; hence, HKCU is usually left empty.

Should the environment variable PYTHONHOME be already set up, it can be taken as "Python Home." Otherwise, the primary Python executable's path would be used to find a "landmark file" — Lib\os.py to figure out the "Python Home." Should it find a Python home, all the subdirectories relevant to it and included in the sys.path such as plat-win, Lib, among others, are according to the folder. Conversely, the core Python path is formed using the PYTHONPATH saved into the registry.

In the case that it cannot find the Python Home, there would be no defined PYTHONPATH in the environment. Conversely, when no registry entries can be located, a default path containing associated entries is utilized instead. For example, \Lib;.\plat-win, etcetera.

The eventual output of this process is given as:

When Python.exe or other .exe are being executed using the Python leading directory (either from the PC build directory directly or on an installed version), the core path can be deduced. At the same time, those in the registry are left unused. The other "application paths" found in a registry are always read.

When another .exe is used to host Python (say, embedded through a COM, placed in a different directory, etcetera), the "Python Home" would be left unreduced; hence, the core path stemming from the registry is utilized instead. In this case the other "application paths" in the registry are read at all times.

Should Python be unable to locate its home, and there is an apparent absence of a registry, say, from frozen .exe or any other absurd set up during installation, you would receive a path containing some defaults, albeit relative paths.

- Running Python scripts:

Python scripts are files which contain the .py extension. They are typically executed by default using the Python.exe. The executable raises a terminal which remains unclosed even when the program makes use of a GUI. To avoid such an occurrence, ensure to make use of the extension .pyw, that would make sure the script is run by default with the pythonw.exe (both executables can be found in the top part of the directory of Python installation. During startup, this intervention would suppress the terminal window. You can also try to run all your Python scripts using pythonw.exe by setting it via the normal facilitates, for instance, (administrative rights might be required:

Startup the command prompt environment

Assign the correct file group to the Python scripts:

assoc .py=Python.File

Proceed to redirect every Python file into the newly made executable:

ftype Python.File=C:\Path\to\pythonw.exe "%1" %*

Conclusion

Working in Python can be one of the best programming languages for you to choose. It is simple to use for even the beginner, but it has the true power behind it to make it a great programming language also if you are more of an advanced programmer in the process. There are just so many things that you can do with the Python program, and since you can mix it in with some of the other programming languages, there is almost nothing that you can't do with Python on your side.

It is not a problem if you are really limited to what you can do when using a programming language. Python is an excellent way for you to use to get familiar and to do some amazing things without having to get scared at how all the code will look. But this is not an issue when it comes to using Python because the language has been cleaned up to help everyone read and look at it together.

This book is going to have all the tools that you need to hit the more advanced parts of Python. Whether you are looking at this book because you have a bit of experience using Python and you want to do a few more advanced things, or you are starting as a beginner, you are sure to find the answers that you need in no time. So take a look through this book and find out everything that you need to know to get some great codes while using the Python programming.